PRAISE FOR MINDFUL FUNDRAISING

An important belief of Judeo-Christian doctrine is "To whom much is given, much is required."

In his new book, *Mindful Fundraising*, Sagi Melamed clearly addresses the fundamental concept of "paying it forward." When we have been blessed, we are all called to be a blessing to others accordingly and to share this concept with the world.

I am thankful for both the fundraisers and the donors – each contribute to making our world a better place for all. Those in need should never be afraid to ask for help. Everyone is called to humbly and generously contribute to those in need.

David Steward, *Founder and Chairman, World Wide Technology*

Sagi Melamed takes the mystery and fear out of fundraising with a straightforward, clearly written how-to book. It will be useful not only for the professional starting out, but equally for the volunteer board member who wants to help an organization pull its fundraising act together. It's full of important suggestions as well as examples of how gifts are asked for and achieved. Melamed has done a big favor for the fundraising field and the causes we hold so dear.

Stephen H. Hoffman, *Chairman, Jack, Joseph and Morton Mandel Foundation*

Replete with anecdotes from his own experience and that of a wide range of colleagues, Sagi Melamed's *Mindful Fundraising* offers accessible, engaging, practical advice to professional and volunteer fundraisers. While providing pragmatic guidance on all elements of a fundraising organization, Melamed vibrantly, gratifyingly illustrates the human side of the work and the satisfaction to be had in helping organizations achieve their goals and realize their missions.

Tamara Rogers, *Former Vice President for Alumni Affairs and Development, Harvard University*

Fundraising may be the most underrated profession in the world. Yet it enables private philanthropy, which is the engine for high culture and making a better world. Private philanthropy makes possible new approaches and disruptive creativity. Thanks to private initiatives, new people and new visions can be brought forward to enable transformation of a mediocre status quo to projects of greatness. Pioneering philanthropy brings attention to the neglected and the overlooked; it initiates treatment for the as yet not identified problems and develops solutions. In the end, fundraising makes an infinite number of good projects possible.

In this book, Sagi Melamed introduces us to this neglected profession. With story and wisdom, he teaches people the ropes and guides them on how to make their dreams come true. He explains the priceless value of connecting donors to a cause that will give depth and meaning to their lives. The entire book communicates the nobility of the profession – even as it gives practical and insightful guidelines to the amateur and professional fundraiser alike.

> **Blu Greenberg,** *author of On Women and Judaism and How to Run a Traditional Jewish Household; and* **Yitz Greenberg,** *President of the J.J. Greenberg Institute for the Advancement of Jewish Life*

Sagi Melamed's masterful work, filled with practical advice, comes from years of experience and a unique empathy for the philanthropist. His recommendations are doable because they are tried and tested. Most important, as he demystifies the field of fundraising, he elevates. You will be edified and inspired with confidence, pride of accomplishment, and an eagerness to excel.

> **Perry Davis,** *President, Perry Davis Associates*

At last, a meaningful book on the subject of fundraising. Thank you, Sagi, for writing this invaluable book that will help people worldwide. *Mindful Fundraising* is destined to become a classic on the art and science of resource development.

> **Robert L. Shook,** *New York Times best-selling author*

Passing on wisdom of experience and learning is one of the greatest gifts we can offer each other in a profession. *Mindful Fundraising* is a testament to Sagi Melamed's generous nature as he shares his journey of learning and the lessons of the many fundraisers, donors, and teachers who have impressed upon him during his established career. This is not only a deeply personal reflection on the fundamental principles that make up successful fundraising, but a demonstration of what makes our sector stronger – integrity, authenticity, and resilience to facilitate positive change in the world.

Kim van Niekerk, *fundraising lecturer and consultant, United Kingdom*

Mindful Fundraising is a must-read for anyone involved in fundraising. Sagi Melamed makes the process of raising money clear and accessible to novice and seasoned readers alike. His anecdotes range from humorous to sobering and always offer valuable insight. Sagi is a true professional, and his book provides the reader with unparalleled access to his experience and acuity. Fundraising may never have been as challenging as it is now, and *Mindful Fundraising* is the guide that will benefit anyone in this endeavor.

Larry Smith, *businessman, philanthropist, and Trustee of Suffolk University, Boston*

In *Mindful Fundraising,* Sagi Melamed provides professional and volunteer fundraisers a clear, practical, and immediately useful guide to fundraising. He brings this guidance to life with his own stories and stories of friends around the world, showing us that everyone can be successful at fundraising and that bringing organizations and donors together can be both deeply rewarding and fun. Above all, he reminds us that fundraising is about three Rs: Relationships, Relationships, Relationships. I recommend this book to anyone and everyone who wants to facilitate the generosity of donors and help them make our world a better place.

Ronald J. Schiller, *Founding Partner, Aspen Leadership Group; former Vice President for Alumni Relations and Development, University of Chicago; author of Belief and Confidence: Donors Talk about Successful Philanthropic Partnership*

What is the mindset of the fundraiser toward fulfilling his dream? Is it one of a beggar who sticks out his hand and asks for help? Or the marvel of a visionary, who offers wealthy individuals the opportunity to invest their money with confidence?

Sagi Melamed confronts the reader with the deep insight that the fundraiser must bring to the encounter in order to find a partner in the vision and its implementation. Readers of this book will discover the sensitivity in the work of fundraising and the sense of respect inherent in this profession.

Rabbi Dr. Binyamin Lau, *Founder, 929 Tanakh B'Yachad daily Bible study initiative*

Business entrepreneurship and resource development share many aspects. In both fields, you need the vision and talent to dream and to paint the dream in bright, inspirational colors. You must enlist partners, and you must push to fulfill the dream with professionalism, perseverance, and enthusiasm.

Sagi Melamed skillfully demonstrates the fundamentals of fundraising. This is a must-read for anyone who ever dreamed but did not dare.

Imad Telhami, *Founder and Chairman, Babcom*

I warmly recommend this essential guide, which represents a comprehensive and in-depth compendium of knowledge, theory, and methods in the fundraising field. Anyone who volunteers or works in fundraising understands that they must learn the values and work methods of this field. They must study the use of tools, wise implementation of professional judgment, and the scientific and practical fundamentals of fundraising activity.

This book is written in a friendly, clear format and is enriched with examples and explanations that bring the material alive. I would like to thank Sagi personally for this book, which has been so lacking for us as leaders in this area.

Prof. Eliezer Yaffe, *Hebrew University of Jerusalem*

In *Mindful Fundraising*, Sagi Melamed provides invaluable, practical insights and strategies for both the resource development professional and the anxious volunteer who dreads asking for a gift. He reminds us that charitable fundraising is sacred work, then provides the tools for being effective instruments in furthering the causes in which we believe. If you want to raise your game as a force for *tikkun olam, Mindful Fundraising* is a must-read!

Jeremy Friedman, *businessman and philanthropist, Canada*

Mindful Fundraising

SAGI MELAMED

gefen גפן
publishing house בית הוצאה לאור
JERUSALEM ◆ NEW YORK   Est. 1981

Cover Design: Jaki Levy
Cover illustration: Jaki Levy
Typesetting: Optume Technologies
ISBN: 978-965-229-974-1
1 3 5 7 9 8 6 4 2

Gefen Publishing House Ltd.   Gefen Books
6 Hatzvi Street   c/o Baker & Taylor Publisher Services
Jerusalem 9438614   30 Amberwood Parkway
Israel   Ashland, Ohio 44805
972-2-538-0247   516-593-1234
orders@gefenpublishing.com   orders@gefenpublishing.com

www.gefenpublishing.com

Printed in Israel

Library of Congress Control Number: 2020920934

Contents

FOREWORD

Throughout the world, the profession of fundraising is still at its relative genesis, while at the same time there is a severe shortage of talented, trained professionals in the field of resource development. In his groundbreaking work, Sagi Melamed guides the reader along the path of the art and the science of resource development for social profit organizations. Thanks to his broad experience in the field and willingness to share, Melamed is detailed and informative on the one hand, while thought-provoking and compelling on the other. For these reasons and others, *Mindful Fundraising* is extremely important to everyone who wants to fundraise: when you get to the end of *Mindful Fundraising*, you'll want to go out there and do it yourself.

I have served in various leadership capacities, including CEO of the American Jewish Joint Distribution Committee, one of the largest and oldest global humanitarian organizations in the world. In the four decades that I have been involved in fundraising, I have often found that people relate to it as if it were merely sales. From my viewpoint, fundraising is an educational and inspirational act, in one of its most beautiful expressions: the presentation of a cause and mission to people who have the ability to financially assist others in need. In essence, the fundraiser serves as the voice of the voiceless, assisting the donor in finding deeper existential meaning through the act of giving.

The most inspiring and fulfilling moments in my professional life were those sacred occasions when I was a conduit, a messenger of souls, voices, and communities that were not in the room with us. Is this sales? Perhaps some people might see it as such – but not I. In my view, these fundraising encounters were sacred moments when soul met soul, mission met mission, dream met dream.

This is why the greatest fundraisers are the people who believe deeply in their mission – those who are fully dedicated to the vision and goals of the cause for which they seek support – and they are experts in educating and communicating prescriptively with each donor.

As the world rapidly changes, as the social fabrics of too many countries are tearing at an alarming rate, as a pandemic plagues the world, the field of financial resource development takes on heightened, if not historic, importance. The growth in global wealth coupled with massively increased socioeconomic needs of the most vulnerable among us make this a critically important time for the release of this book. The author brings with him a rich and diversified background that comes through clearly and compellingly in his writing. To put it succinctly, this book includes the right content, is being published at the right time, and is written by a master of the craft.

Reading this book will help leaders to achieve a better understanding of what is needed to drive their organizations forward in a competitive, constantly changing world.

Alan H. Gill, *Executive Vice President Emeritus, American Jewish Joint Distribution Committee*

PREFACE

If you take only one thing from this book, let this be it: you too can fundraise!

"I served as a pilot and senior commander in the Air Force for decades. I led people into combat and back. I shot down seven enemy airplanes. I've stared death in the face, but I've never done anything as difficult and complex as fundraising." This is what retired brigadier general Ran Peker said to me as he talked about the nonprofit organization he had founded to help disadvantaged youth.

I've often heard people say things such as, "I would never be able to ask people for donations!" Or, "How on earth do you do it?" What state of mind do you need to be in to ask for charitable gifts? What does it take to be a good fundraiser? This book intends to answer these questions.

My first fundraising experience was back in 1992, while studying for my BA in Middle Eastern Studies at the University of Haifa, before I even knew the term *fundraising*. While applying to advanced degree programs at top universities in the United States, I realized that beyond good grades and high motivation, the acceptance committees were looking for extracurriculars – unique, innovative activities. So I decided to make an old dream come true. I would combine my passion for karate with my academic studies and practice my newly acquired Arabic language skills along the way. I contacted a friend from the Bedouin village of Khawaled and offered to start a karate program for the village children.

At that time, the concept of extracurricular activities was completely unknown in Khawaled and probably most Bedouin villages. After school, the children would walk on a dirt road back to the tin huts and sheds that they called home. They would help their parents herd the goats and work the fields.

At best, they might play ball games in a dusty field. The concept of organized weekly lessons wearing white karate outfits was revolutionary for these kids.

My Bedouin friend Khaldi recruited the support of the village teacher, who was known by the honorary title "the Teacher." Together they put together a list of some twenty boys and girls who were interested in learning karate. There was only one problem. Where would we teach them? The village didn't even have a spare mobile classroom where we could set up a karate school. As there was no other option, we decided to bus the kids to the gym of the local regional council, about four miles away. The mayor of the regional council offered to subsidize the cost of renting the gym. I volunteered my time for the instruction. But we were still short the $5,000 to pay for a special bus twice a week throughout the year. What should we do?

At the time, my wife Betsy was working as a research assistant at Oranim Academic College, and she told me about an American foundation, the Abraham Fund, which supported projects for coexistence between Jews and Arabs. Perhaps they would be willing to help these Bedouin kids?

I wrote a letter to the fund, explaining our situation. Two weeks later, I received a reply from the director, Joan Bronk: "Your project sounds interesting. We've already completed our funding allocations for this year, but if you happen to be in New York, I'd be happy to meet with you and hear more."

That summer, we traveled to Connecticut to visit Betsy's parents. I wrote to Ms. Bronk that I would take the train to New York to meet her. When I arrived, the office was practically deserted. Most of the employees were on vacation. Here I was, a stubborn kibbutznik full of chutzpah, who had come determined to realize his dream to help twenty Bedouin kids in a tiny village that wasn't even on the map. Right there on the carpet of her fancy Manhattan office, I gave Ms. Bronk a martial arts demonstration and explained how teaching these kids karate would contribute to promoting coexistence between Jews and Arabs. To this day, I'm not sure what she thought about the unsophisticated Israeli's unusual fundraising campaign, but a few weeks later, I received confirmation of a contribution from the Abraham Fund. That's how the karate class for the kids of Khawaled became a reality.

A few years later, I had the privilege of seeing one of the village girls from the very first class receive her black belt. This was also my first step into the world of fundraising.

In the early 2000s, Betsy and I realized that there was a need for resource development consulting among nonprofits in Israel. By then, Betsy already had a reputation as an excellent fundraiser due to her success in raising money for a religious educational institution in the northern part of Israel.

Because of this success, we would get a call to our home every week or so from leaders of nonprofit organizations, asking Betsy whether she could help them with their fundraising efforts. These organizations were of diverse types: religious seminaries, educational institutions, after-school youth empowerment programs, sports teams, environmental organizations, and even a pair of bereaved parents who wanted to commemorate their son who was killed in battle.

When we became aware that this need existed, that organizations were willing to pay for consulting and support (though not always enough, as we'll discuss later), and that we were both skilled in this work, liked it, and were good at it, we founded our own consulting firm, MASIG.

We had two main principles that guided our work. First, that the best fundraiser for any organization is someone who works within the organization itself. This must be someone who lives and breathes the organization, who wakes up every morning thinking about how it can be improved and who spends every day striving for its success. The second principle was that the knowledge, experience, and relationships acquired through fundraising work must stay within the organization, rather than being garnered by some external company. These two principles stood in opposition to the natural tendency of many organizations that were very keen to raise funds but didn't know "how it's done." These organizations would instead seek to outsource their resource development to external fundraising companies, which operate as "guns for hire" rather than as an organic part of the organization itself.

This book is based on the experience we accumulated over years of resource development on behalf of various organizations for which we worked or volunteered, and on thousands of consulting hours with dozens of other organizations in the process of establishing, developing, or upgrading their fundraising strategy and operations. It includes excerpts from multiple interviews I conducted with fundraising experts from all over the world, as well as numerous real-life anecdotes about the fundraising experience from all sides of the table. Note that many names have been changed to protect the privacy of the individuals concerned.

The book is intended for a broad audience of readers, including:

- Directors and presidents of nonprofits
- Nonprofit board members and lay leaders
- Resource development professionals
- Social activists and social entrepreneurs
- Anyone else with an interest – professional or otherwise – in learning about the art and science of fundraising

The book does not contain lists of foundations and potential donors who can be approached for funding. Absolutely not. This is one of the first rules of our consulting work at MASIG – we don't give names, we give tools. We train our consultees in how to build and nurture their own lists of names.

If you take only one thing from this book, let this be it: you too can successfully fundraise!

Over the years, I've met only a handful of people for whom asking for a donation from someone else comes easy. These are the rare few who can look another person straight in the eye and say confidently and without missing a beat: "I'd like to invite you to make a significant change in the lives of children at risk/students at this institution/single-parent mothers/asylum seekers/cancer patients/the people of the Middle East/whoever, by giving a donation of $X, that will allow us to do Y…"

In my efforts to train leaders of organizations in resource development work, I've seen time and again how even the most talented people – smart, innovative, charismatic, and adored professionals – find it hard to ask for donations.

Rabbi David is the head of a yeshiva (religious seminary) who is admired and loved by all who know him. If he asks for something, it's hard to say no. I was working with him on a simulation exercise of asking for a contribution from a potential donor, and he did an excellent job of describing the institution he founded and led, clearly explaining the challenges facing the moderate religious movement and singing the praises of his many students. But when the time came for him to utter the words "ask for a donation," in some form or other, he started to squirm in his chair, smile awkwardly, and abruptly change the subject. He just couldn't come out and ask for money. He was like a basketball player who could dribble around opponents for fun, but just couldn't put the ball in the basket. We needed to do a lot of one-on-one work together for him to be able to sink the ball, but once he got used to the idea and practiced doing it, he could slam-dunk like a pro.

Danny is a social entrepreneur and an internationally recognized karate master. He founded Budo for Peace, a nonprofit promoting harmony, peaceful conflict resolution, and Jewish-Arab coexistence using martial arts as a common set of values and language. After he'd recruited me to the organization's board of directors, Danny would sometimes ask for my help with fundraising matters.

Danny has a winning personality. He's a gentle, humble soul with great inner strength, creativity, and charisma. He also has access to the upper echelons of the business world and the public sector in Israel. Moreover, Budo for Peace is a unique organization worldwide and gets an enthusiastic reaction from almost everyone who hears about its activities. It has an original and thought-provoking approach of using physically aggressive and strenuous martial arts as a means to reduce violence and promote a more tolerant shared society.

Despite all these advantages, and despite having met with many potential donors who were open to hearing about the needs of Budo for Peace, Danny struggled to raise funds for the organization he'd founded and which had gradually become his life's work. Though he and his wife themselves gave generously to the organization, he couldn't bring himself to ask anyone else for donations.

At one of our many meetings, Danny presented me with an urgent need for funding. He was organizing a joint Arab-Jewish delegation from Budo for Peace to the World Karate Championships, being held in Australia. To cover expenses, he needed $4,000 for each participant, but the delegation was now in jeopardy due to lack of funds. "What do you think?" he asked me. "How can we raise the money we need in just a week?"

"Danny, you yourself are the answer," I replied. "You have to prepare a short and interesting bio of every member of the delegation to the World Karate Championships, with a picture of the kid. Pick up the phone to some of your acquaintances who can donate $4,000 without too much trouble. Ask to meet with them, or at least to talk with them over the phone. Persuade each of them to 'adopt' one of these participants, explaining that their donation will enable this young person to compete in the championships. They won't be able to turn you away empty-handed." And I added: "The time factor is actually an advantage. You have to do this in the next two days. The pressure will help make sure you get it done. You just can't put it off any longer."

And he did it. A few days later, Danny proudly told me how five different people had answered his request and donated the necessary funds, and that the delegation would now be able to travel to the championships.

"Danny, you've just broken the fear barrier to asking for a donation. From now on, you just need to do the same thing again and again. It's like breaking a wooden board with a karate chop. Once you've proved to yourself that you can do it, the next time it becomes a whole lot easier."

In other words, anyone can fundraise! Some people find it the most natural thing in the world. For most, it doesn't come easy. But with the right training and empowerment, and by changing your preconceptions and removing the barriers that are holding you back, you can do it too!

I hope you find this book both engaging and useful. I'd be delighted to hear your thoughts and insights, and your own fundraising stories.

Sagi Melamed
Melamed.Sagi@gmail.com

CHAPTER 1

Fundraising – Past, Present, and Future

Fundraising in this day and age can essentially be boiled down to "motivating and inviting people to fulfill a dream while inspiring them to use their money to do good."

My friend Chuck Ratner of Cleveland told me how in the 1960s, Pinchas Sapir, my grandmother's brother, would visit his father Max Ratner to ask for a donation to the nascent Jewish state. Pinchas would sit in Max's living room with his feet up on the couch, and he wouldn't move from the couch until Max had signed a fat check or committed to establishing another factory in Israel's poor, undeveloped periphery.

When Sapir became chairman of the Jewish Agency, the nonprofit organization responsible for bringing funding to the new Jewish state, that simple method continued to work just fine for him and the other fundraisers of his generation in convincing Diaspora Jews to open their hearts and wallets. During that period, on the eve of Israel's founding and during the first few decades of its existence, it was enough to combine the words *Holocaust* and *Jewish state* with the expression "all Jews are responsible for one another." Jews felt that they had an obligation to give, without asking for business plans, measures of success, financial reports, or pooling of resources.

As in many other fields, standards of measurement and styles of resource development have changed. The previous generation of Diaspora Jews either personally experienced the Holocaust or knew survivors. Their dying wish was to visit the Land of Israel. They had dreamed of an independent state for the Jews and watched proudly as this dream came true. Show them a photo of a Jewish soldier carrying a gun and wearing the uniform of the Israel Defense Forces, and they saw a messianic vision. They understood that the State of Israel offered Jews all around the world a new hope of living without fear, in safety and pride. But this generation has gradually made way for a new one. In addition, the rules have changed in the world of philanthropy.

Jay Ruderman, President of the Ruderman Family Foundation, which is involved in advancing awareness and understanding of the American Jewish community among Israeli decision makers, explained to me the reasons for the gradual decrease in support for Israel by American Jews:

> Take me and my family, for example. My parents were born in the late 1930s. They witnessed the Holocaust, the establishment of the State of Israel, and the Six-Day War. But my generation takes the Jewish state for granted – a state that's mainly known to the world for an endless chain of violent conflict. We witnessed the First and Second Lebanon Wars and the Intifadas. What's more, my parents' generation had little familiarity with institutions in the United States, whether hospitals, universities, or sports clubs. The elite universities like Harvard and Yale had quotas for Jewish students. This discrimination created a closed, united Jewish community. But today, Jews are everywhere, at the highest levels of society and in leadership positions. The Jews are well integrated in American society, but it comes at a price – the price of assimilation, of distance from Jewish identity. This means that donations are diverted from Jewish institutions to non-Jewish causes.

Furthermore, modern Israel has achieved economic stability, boasting Nobel Prize winners and scientific breakthroughs. It has become the "start-up nation," with hundreds of homegrown millionaires. In parallel, the expectations of Diaspora Jews from their Israeli counterparts have grown – and they are expected to give as well. "How much are the Israelis giving?" has become the most popular question in the world of fundraising abroad for Israeli institutions.

Noam Lautman, Chairman of the Lautman Foundation and a member of Committed to Give, an initiative to increase the number of philanthropic givers in Israel, also mentioned this issue when I spoke to him:

When we step up and motivate Israelis to donate to nonprofits, we explain to them that every shekel they donate in Israel is worth twice its value, as it helps raise funds from overseas donors. Israeli organizations that don't have Israeli donors have a hard time raising money overseas.

I have identified a positive trend of awareness and an increase in donations made by Israelis, but we are still far from where we should be. Committed to Give found that out of about 130,000 Israelis who have at least a million dollars "extra," about 2,600 of them donate a sum of at least 50,000 shekels a year. Our goal is to substantially increase that figure.

James Snyder, CEO of the Israel Museum, gave me an accurate description of the development of a philanthropic culture in Israel:

> Israel is a new state in an ancient location. Not very long ago, there was no money to give and nowhere to give it. Israel was established as a socialist country, and a philanthropic culture, as we know it today, was not one of the state's main values. This picture is gradually changing. Israelis with capital are following the example of their counterparts overseas, and philanthropy is slowly becoming part of Israeli culture as well.

THE RISE OF INDIVIDUALISM AND THE INFORMATION REVOLUTION

The late twentieth century and early twenty-first exhibit a clear trend of individualism – less "we," more "I." More "what's in it for me" and less "what does this contribute to my community/country." Sixty years ago, John F. Kennedy said the immortal words "Ask not what your country can do for you – ask what you can do for your country." This was moving at the time, but hardly reflects the dominant ethos today.

The field of philanthropy is also influenced by the accessibility of information. As opposed to the acceptable modus vivendi in the not-so-distant past, today it's almost impossible to hoodwink donors. Organizations can't get away with promising the moon but not delivering or hiding a mediocre reality behind a fancy façade. Today in just a few minutes, anyone equipped with a smartphone can search the net and make calls to find information that used to take weeks to unearth, if it could be found at all.

The combination of these trends – individualism and information explosion – poses a challenge for fundraising experts. It forces them to adapt the organization's objectives to the goals, dreams, and needs of the donor. In parallel, they must improve professionalism by verifying transparency and reliability, giving the donor reliable and accurate information, and avoiding cutting corners. The attitude of "It doesn't matter, the donor doesn't know what it's for anyway" has no place in today's fundraising scene.

I've heard countless sad stories of organizations and fundraisers who promised and didn't fulfill, made commitments and didn't stick by them, tried to cut corners and were caught, sold the same project to numerous donors, removed a donor sign from a building after the donation was received, and so on… Each time this happens, I'm sorry to have to hear an organization getting slammed by a justifiably angry and frustrated donor. It's hard to build a good reputation, but so easy to ruin it. As the Jewish Sages said in *Ethics of the Fathers*, "A good name is better than fine oil."

Donor preference for designated donations, along with the rising trend of donating to organizations in a field close to the donor's heart, means that donations are shrinking to the major umbrella organizations of the Jewish community.

But some believe that eventually this trend will change. One is Shoel Silver of Toronto, businessman and philanthropist, who has served as Chairman of the Jewish Agency for Israel's Budget and Finance Committee and President of the United Israel Appeal of Canada. He asserts:

> I understand the generation of young donors in their thirties and forties, who want to give to specific issues that they support and are less enthusiastic about supporting large community organizations. But at the same time, I hope and believe that in another fifteen to twenty years, they'll realize that when everyone donates only to the organization that's important to them, it's very difficult to build and maintain a Jewish community. I anticipate that they will change their donation preferences and return to believing in the unique value and

importance of collective responsibility, both on the local Jewish level and on the level of Klal Yisrael – the entire Jewish people. Motivated by this belief, I trust that they will choose to invest in large Jewish community organizations.

Shoel Silver's words, shared several years before the COVID-19 pandemic, became a prophecy when COVID-19 hit Canada (and the rest of the world) in the spring of 2020. UJA's Emergency Campaign for Community Resilience raised about $29 million from the Jewish community of Toronto to save many Jewish social service agencies. This community-wide campaign, led by the Jewish Federation of Toronto, raised money to help vulnerable members of the community battle depression, anxiety, job loss, isolation, and addiction, all challenges that have worsened during this difficult time.

TRANSPARENCY AND PROFESSIONALISM

Another trend in the field is the involvement of donors in implementing their donations and the plans they support. In the past, donors would give millions of dollars to major organizations such as hospitals, museums, botanical gardens, and the like, confident that the staff would "know what best to do with my money." They would visit the organization once every few years and enjoy seeing their names etched on the wall, hear organization executives sing their praises, and view new art exhibitions all made possible with their donations. Of course, every rule has its exceptions, but in general, those days are no longer.

Today, most donors, and particularly the major ones, want information and transparency, including financial reports, evaluation of targets, a long-term sustainability plan (what happens when I stop giving?). They demand criteria for measuring success, architectural plans, and even direct contact with the final beneficiaries of the donation, which may include parents of children with cancer, schoolchildren during their visit to the botanical gardens, and any other direct or indirect recipient.

This is not to say that donor involvement is identical for every donor and in every situation. The level of involvement, detail, and demand for reports and data changes in each situation. But the fundraiser must be willing and able to provide the data on time, in a professional manner, and with full transparency and honesty.

Donor expectations for more involvement and transparency mean that the organization's managers and resource development professionals must practice proficient management. Information must be reliable, updated, and readily available. This can be done by tailoring reports to the donor, supplying an annual report, or putting this information on the website. Reporting must be exact and well formulated. Donor visits to the organizations must be focused and efficiently coordinated. Smart use of technology such as websites, video clips, and social media enable maintaining a reliable, continuous connection with the donor.

Additional professionalism is required from the less well known organizations – the ones who aren't household brands. When I began my position as Vice President of Resource Development at Tel Hai College, I repeated to my colleagues: "An Ivy League university can sometimes permit itself to cut corners, to be a bit sloppy. Everyone will still believe that it's an excellent university. Tel Hai College can't allow itself to work carelessly."

Professionalism not only applies to how the organization is presented, but also to how the organization's management presents themselves. Let's talk dress code. I once heard a savvy, extremely well dressed and nattily groomed fundraising professional from Baltimore brief his group of fundraisers. "Your job," he emphasized, "is your donor's hobby. Therefore, you need to be professionally dressed and presentable even when your donor is dressed in shorts and a T-shirt. You are at work; his philanthropy, even though it's serious business, is his play." Potential donors often arrive for site visits and other events in informal attire. In Israel, it is not uncommon for the donor to arrive wearing shorts, a T-shirt, and sandals. It's tempting for the hosts to dress similarly when with donors, but this is not acceptable. Donors can permit themselves to dress casually, but the fundraiser can't. As the saying goes, "If you want to raise a million dollars, you have to look like a million dollars."

This doesn't mean you have to invest in expensive, showy marketing materials or wear thousand-dollar designer suits. The marketing materials, the refreshments served, the gift you leave behind should all be adapted to the location and status of the organization – but they should always be respectable and appropriate. The fundraiser's clothing should reflect the same principle – it must be clean, pressed, appropriate to location and situation, and respectable. A $200 suit that looks neat is perfectly fine – much better than a suit left over from a nephew's wedding that you retrieved from the mothballs, dress shoes with worn soles, a belt that has known better days, and a tie from the kids' dress-up box. Don't laugh, we've seen it all!

VISION, DREAM, AND THE PATH TO ACHIEVING THEM

To solicit donations is sometimes called in Yiddish to *schnorr* – meaning "beg" or "flatter" – a word that bears a whiff of the old Jewish towns in Europe or of Charles Dickens's London in *Oliver Twist* or even of the New York City subway. Those who consider fundraising activity to be the work of a schnorrer or beggar will never go far. Even more importantly, they will not enjoy the attempt.

Fundraising and development, as I see it, is about vision and dream. Fundraisers must believe in the cause for which they are raising money and must be capable of translating the organization's physical and fiscal needs into a vision and a dream. A fundraiser who treats his or her work as *begging* and views donation requests as requests for personal favors from the donors will never succeed. Fundraising in this day and age can essentially be boiled down to "motivating and inviting people to fulfill a dream while inspiring them to use their money to do good."

I was able to express this worldview during my term as Vice President of Tel Hai College in northern Israel on the border of Lebanon. In 2009, we dedicated a new campus for the college in the foothills of snow-capped Mount Hermon. During the fundraising campaign for the new campus, I used to say that most of our work was already done for us by God. The stunning scenery of the Upper Galilee was more convincing than the most polished presentation or dazzling marketing brochure.

During the dedication ceremony for the Jewish-Arab Center for Democracy on the new campus, donors Debbie Eisenberg and Gary Levene of Canada got up to say a few words. In the presence of Israel's President Shimon Peres and many other honored guests, Debbie and Gary had tears in their eyes as they expressed their thanks – to me, for inviting and encouraging them a few years earlier to invest their money in this important project, which was so vital to the Galilee region, Israeli society, and the State of Israel. They spoke about the satisfaction they felt from their involvement in the college, the warm connection between us, and the privilege they had gained in donating to such an important project.

It was a magical moment for me. Debbie and Gary's emotional expression of joy in their donation together with the respect that I felt for them all along the process was the perfect reward for the long days and nights I had invested in searching for and inviting potential donors to the new campus, exhausting flights around the world, dozens of negative answers to my requests, and many frustrations on the challenging path of fundraising.

The truth is, it's hard to draw a clear line between schnorring and resource development. The main difference between the two seems to be the attitude, the perception of the role. I learned an important lesson about this at an early stage in my resource development career from the late Professor Michael Hammer.

During the 1990s, I was in Boston studying for a master's degree at Harvard. My wife was working at CJP, the Boston Jewish Federation. At that time, the classic fundraising model of the Jewish Federations in the United States was based on a team of community volunteers. These volunteers are given pledge cards with names of past and potential donors, according to their level of experience and status. They work under the supervision of a Federation fundraiser, who directs ongoing professional training and provides support.

One evening, we attended a training and appreciation event at which Michael Hammer was the keynote speaker. Until his untimely death in 2008 at the age of sixty, Michael taught at MIT and was considered a world expert on management. His book *Reengineering the Corporation* was considered a groundbreaking guide to a new theory in the business management industry. In his speech to the volunteers, Michael said the following words, which still guide me today: "When you ask for a donation, don't feel like the donor is doing you a favor – rather, the opposite is true: you're doing him a favor by helping him to do something good with his money." I found a similar statement in the Jewish sources: "The donation benefits the giver more than it benefits the receiver" (*Leviticus Rabbah* 34:9). This attitude toward fundraising is the fundamental difference between the beggar and the resource development professional or volunteer.

In the following chapters, we'll learn how to do it right.

CHAPTER 2

WHY DO ORGANIZATIONS NEED TO RAISE MONEY?

Correct, successful fundraising must be driven by a vision. There must be a dream waiting to be realized. Fundraising is the tool for realizing the organization's vision.

Why is fundraising necessary? Why do organizations invest time, thought, and resources in fundraising? We can identify several main reasons for this:

A. To exist. Thousands of nonprofit organizations would not be able to exist without the philanthropic support they receive. Nonprofits sometimes have a government budget or income generated from activities, but these are usually not enough to support their basic needs. Without donations, they would not exist. These organizations have no choice but to invest in resource development, and it is particularly vital for them to establish a stable and efficient fundraising mechanism.

B. To keep surviving. Sometimes I receive desperate requests from nonprofits. "We have to get donations, otherwise we're in danger of extinction!" The reasons vary. Some rely on government funding that was slashed. Sometimes, they have relied on a small number of donors or even one major donor, and these have pulled out. Others have fallen into debt due to financial mismanagement. In any case, an emergency situation is the worst time to start fundraising activity. This is like remembering that you need a source of water when you're in the middle of a hike in the desert. We'll discuss this more later.

C. To grow. Some say that nonprofit organizations are overly reliant on donations. Recent years witness an increased awareness of the need to create income sources beyond donations, such as payment for services, know-how, or products, creating relationships with industry, and integrating business with social goals (social enterprise). Every nonprofit must obtain donations – to expand existing programs and develop new ones, grant financial aid and scholarships to those who need the help, and also to build or rent space for organizational growth.

D. Infrastructure for a rainy day. Some directors are like Joseph in the Book of Genesis, who stored grain in advance of the famine – they wisely develop fundraising activities during the full and plenty years of the organization, aware that this situation will not last forever. A smart organization acts with foresight and develops sources of funding for the future, thereby reinforcing its sustainability.

When Israeli windsurfer Gal Friedman won the first-ever Olympic gold medal for Israel in the Athens 2004 Olympics, a Jewish businessman from Florida was so excited that Israel had finally received a gold medal that he donated $10 million to a national Israeli sports organization. This record-breaking gift was used for about ten years to promote and support competitive athletes. After a decade, the gift was depleted. Only then did the organization wake up and realize that they had to start building fundraising capacity in order to receive new gifts. As I advised the organization on building a fundraising organization, I wished they had called me sooner: the best time to start planning for the future is long before your resources are drained.

E. Have we mentioned self-esteem? As in many other areas of life, success in fundraising is also important for the psychic well-being of those involved. This applies to the organization's management, board of directors, staff, and of course the fundraisers themselves. A sporting mentality is a requirement in this profession. As in long-distance running or a baseball playoff game, there are moments of failure alongside moments of success. Some of the ability to get up and keep running after a fall comes from a strong and healthy sense of self, which pushes a person to keep going with all her might.

FUNDRAISING MODELS FOR ORGANIZATIONS

The activity and goals of fundraising are identical whether performed in a small nonprofit organization with five staff members or a major university or hospital. It boils down to forming a vision and inspiring people to connect to it and support it.

That said, there are major differences between fundraising for a small organization as opposed to a large one, or for one that was just created versus long-standing institutions that have been around for decades. Some organizations benefit (and sometimes suffer) from Friends groups, and others carry out all fundraising from their headquarters; some have fundraising staffs of over a hundred, and sometimes it's just one lonely CEO of a nonprofit who has to fundraise all by himself while simultaneously managing the organization.

I will now define several unique characteristics, main challenges, and the resulting needs of fundraising activity in a number of types of organizations, divided by size and age. Of course, this division is artificial, and within the groups there are significant differences and varied needs.

Fundraising in Start-Up Nonprofits

A start-up can be a nonprofit in the first few years of activity. It can also be an older organization that previously managed without organized fundraising, or one that was not successful in fundraising in the past and decided to begin to do it now. Below are several challenges involved in establishing a fundraising mechanism in a nonprofit start-up:

1. Most of the required actions (defining a vision, preparing marketing materials, establishing Friends groups) must be carried out simultaneously, and by a very small staff.
2. The start-up is usually unknown, globally, nationally, or even locally. It must create name recognition quickly, so that potential donors will be able to identify with it. This is not necessarily only a challenge – sometimes it's also an opportunity. Many long-standing organizations have to deal with a negative image and invest vast resources in improving their reputations. Sometimes it's an advantage to be the new kid on the block.

3.   The start-up lacks (or has a limited number of) donors and supporters who can serve as a volunteer team for recruiting new donors. Individuals who have a tradition of giving to an organization are an excellent starting point for expanding the donor circle, and their absence demands action to create a preliminary donor base.

4.   The start-up lacks continuous income from donations. This would give it a financial basis and economic stability, which in turn enables it to invest the required resources in expanding fundraising activity. In my consulting work, I emphasize the following rule of thumb to the management of non-profit start-ups that want to establish new fundraising mechanisms: *during the first two years, be prepared to invest more money in funding the creation and operation of fundraising operation than the total donations received.* In other words, for about two years, fundraising will cost you money! This is a conservative estimate – if you operate correctly and recruit the right person, sometimes just one year is enough to return the investment. But the rule stands: raising money costs money, and you must be prepared for this and equipped with patience – both financial and mental.

5.   Often, new nonprofits are established through a significant donation of a specific donor or fund that wishes to advance a certain agenda or handle a certain challenge. They invest their money, time, and energy in founding a nonprofit dedicated to addressing this issue. Relying on a single donor may make the manager's job significantly easier (you only have to please and report to one person), but it also represents a risk for the organization's financial sustainability. Reducing or ceasing the donation from the single donor may lead to financial disaster for the organization. Almost always, the single donor will aspire and push to establish a fundraising operation. Assuming that it succeeds, this will increase the number of donors and the nonprofit's income from donations. In turn, the original donor may reward such fundraising efforts with an increase in his or her own gifts.

Fundraising in a Small Organization

In Israel, a small nonprofit organization may number anywhere from just one to twenty individuals (depending on the type of organization and field of activity). In Canada, for example, three-quarters of the small nonprofits have fewer than ten employees. The uniqueness of the small organization for fundraising is defined in the following points:

1. The CEO must carry out most or all the fundraising tasks. Often, one of the major tasks in the job description is fundraising. A potential nonprofit CEO must demonstrate both ability and experience in this area. In some cases, the CEO is able to jumpstart the fundraising operation, but rarely will he or she be able to keep up with all that needs to be done.
2. The organization's budget is relatively small and doesn't have any extra resources to pay a professional fundraiser. Most small organizations are unable to fund a full-time or even half-time position for a fundraiser. Therefore, the CEO often identifies a talented person from within the organization who is already fulfilling another function and adds the task of fundraising to her job description. This usually doesn't work either. It's difficult to find people who are skilled at fundraising, much less when they were hired for their skill or proficiency in a different role that already takes up their time. Furthermore, the CEO is often unwilling or unable to fundraise and gives the task to another employee for that reason. Releasing the CEO from the task of fundraising is a mistake. Another individual can assist the CEO in scheduling meetings, preparing material, presenting reports, and administrative work. But in a small organization, requesting funding from a donor or foundation is the responsibility of the "face" or the top leader of the organization. The CEO is the individual who represents decision-making power and is the go-to person to make sure the donation or funding is being used for the intended purpose. Often a donor would be happy to meet the people who are out in the field, but when discussing money, it is usually the CEO or professional fundraiser with whom they feel most comfortable.
3. Due to the reasons presented above, there is a tendency in small organizations to search for fundraising solutions outside the organization, through outsourcing. Fundraising consulting firms offer to do most of the fundraising work for nonprofits, with an emphasis on preparing requests for donations and sending them to their list of foundations, as well as running an annual online campaign or gala event. In the best case, they work on the basis of a monthly retainer, and in the less ideal case, they take

commission on the total donations. This isn't the right solution for most organizations, unrelated to their size, for reasons I will discuss later.

4. When it becomes possible to hire a professional fundraiser, and a decision is made to do so, a small organization will have difficulty paying the salary necessary to hire an experienced person who can get the job done. Many organizations, challenged to find the right person who will bring them the hoped-for results, are forced to compromise. This is one of the reasons for the high turnover in this profession – the gap between high expectations and disappointing results.

For a small nonprofit to prepare properly for fundraising, the CEO must have the ability and talent to work on this issue personally and to spearhead the fundraising work. Freelance writers, graphic designers, and translators can provide a professional solution for preparing marketing materials, project proposals, and reports. This way the organization avoids having to recruit new personnel for these tasks, preserving its ability to expand and reduce activity based on its needs. A CEO who is armed with a fundraising plan and calendar will be able to maintain a high level of communication with potential donors and supporters and can tap the skilled resources to respond in a timely and professional manner.

Resource Development in a Medium-Sized Organization

Any medium-sized organization (from several dozen up to two hundred individuals, depending on the type of organization and field of activity) with a budget that depends fully or partially on donations must have at least one person whose job is to raise funds. The size of a fundraising team depends on several variables:

1. **Level of dependence on donations.** As an organization's dependence on donations rises, it is obliged to invest more in fundraising.
2. **Success in fundraising.** With success comes the security and confidence to invest more resources in fundraising activity and in the team.
3. **Geographical scope of the fundraising.** As operations spread to other cities, nationally or abroad, the need arises to reinforce the team. This applies to the fundraiser and the supporting staff.

4. **Fundraising tradition.** An organization that successfully solicits donations over many years will maintain a larger staff than one that is taking
   its first steps in the fundraising world.
5. **Organizational culture.** Some organizations take a very focused approach
   to fundraising, while others prefer to cast a wide net. The size and type of
   team required can vary depending on the resource development professionals' work style and personality.

While in start-ups and small organizations, fundraising is carried out by the
CEO and other employees who also carry out other roles, in a medium-sized
organization and certainly a large one, the cost-benefit ratio must be considered. In the Jewish Federations, Israeli universities that raise money internationally, and organizations with a fundraising tradition, the usual expectation
is that the cost of obtaining donations should not exceed about 20 percent of
the total income from donations. Of course, this number isn't set in stone.
It depends on fluctuations in the market, national and global crises (such as
the 2008 financial crisis and the 2020 COVID-19 crisis), the organization's
fiscal status, and targeted campaigns. In addition, this ratio depends on what
is called "bookkeeping intelligence" – how and where you record the numbers
to obtain the desired accounting results. Large organizations with a fundraising tradition often have endowments, which increase the income from donations annually and provide funding for some of the expenses involved.

This can also be built gradually. For example, when I established a resource
development department in a college in northern Israel, my goal for the first
two years was for the sum of donations to exceed the sum of the fundraising
operation's expenses. After we achieved this goal, I set another, more ambitious one: over the next two years, the cost of fundraising would not exceed
25 percent of the total donations received. Simultaneously, I presented the
long-term goal toward which we aspired: average yearly fundraising expenses
would be less than 20 percent of income from donations.

Fundraising in a Large Organization
In a large organization, a fundraising operation is usually institutionalized in
the form of a permanently staffed department with as many as dozens of local
employees. In certain cases, such as the resource development departments of

leading universities, museums, environmental organizations, and hospitals, these operations number hundreds of employees around the world.

As opposed to a small-scale fundraising system, large resource development systems have a clearer division of roles, specializations, and geographical regions of responsibility. For example, in university resource development divisions, we may find desk managers who are in charge of donors and alumni in specific countries and continents; writers of project proposals, reports, and marketing materials; a visits coordinator; website and social media managers; Friends manager; donor appreciation coordinator; database administrator; and more.

THE ORGANIZATION TOMORROW

Correct, successful fundraising must be driven by a vision. There must be a dream waiting to be realized. Fundraising is the tool for realizing the organization's vision. Correct fundraising is like a vivid dream, and donors and partners are those who help bring it to life.

Here's a story. When the Second Lebanon War erupted in the summer of 2006, the Israeli public and Jewish donors worldwide discovered the importance of the Galilee and the need to reinforce Israel's northern border region. Tel Hai College was a growing academic institution that suddenly found itself in the eye of the storm of Hezbollah rocket fire. We competed for the attention and resources of the donors, since we knew that it wouldn't last for long after the rocket blasts died down. But we had one obvious advantage over most of our competitors: we had a plan for the organization tomorrow, titled "the Upper Galilee Development Triangle." This was a $100 million plan whose focus was the construction of a new college campus. Thanks to it, we were able to raise tens of millions of dollars and build a new, much needed and now heavily used campus and new student dormitories. Connections that we made with donors during those years continue to serve the college even years later.

Without a plan, you are fundraising for projects instead of realizing a clear, exciting vision. Or, in the best-case scenario, you are fundraising for exciting but isolated projects. They lack a common link that makes them part of a bigger picture. A stimulating vision is not just a good way to excite your donors. It's important for exciting the management of the organization and the fundraisers as well. When a person is enthusiastic about an idea, it's contagious and radiates outward.

Leaderships of NGOs will often be surprised to discover that they already have the main ingredients for cooking up their plan for the organization tomorrow. These ingredients include activity statistics, participation numbers, physical development plans, projects they would like to advance and expand, and so on. In a nutshell, this plan is composed of three main parts:

1. **What is our current situation?** This looks at the number of participants, personnel, branches, types of activities, physical infrastructure, budgets, achievements and failures, supporters and partners, comparison with other players in the market where we operate, and more, depending on the types of activities.
2. **Where do we want to be in three/five/ten years?** In terms of quantity and quality (regarding the types of information listed above), values, rate of growth, our situation and status in comparison with others in the market (the competition), expansion of areas of operation, and more.
3. **What do we need to do to get from A to B?** This is the meat of the fundraising plan. The resources we need to raise (money, as well as other resources such as volunteers, participants, property and more) are what we need in order to realize the vision of the organization tomorrow.

In this way, the various projects (donation opportunities) are each pieces of the full picture (the organization tomorrow), not just nice activities that are each important on their own. Reaching the multiyear goals described in the plan for the organization tomorrow will probably involve high costs of tens or even hundreds of millions of dollars, depending on the organization. But because the plan is modular and composed of different activities and projects, donations can be raised for each part separately.

CHAPTER 3

THE ART OF THE ASK

"You need to think and feel like you are the one doing the donor a favor, and not the other way around."

In training for karate (and other martial arts), one of the exercises involves breaking a wooden board. The purpose of this exercise is to test the karateka and the strength of his blow, as well as his ability to concentrate the right amount of power in his technique, at the right time, place, and speed. Breaking a board with your bare hand is quite frightening, and I have seen people break their fingers attempting to do it. Their mental preparedness is vital to their success, as the key to breaking the board is confidence that they will be successful.

Guided imagery is used to prepare someone for breaking a board. The karateka must imagine, step by step, the way that he will succeed in breaking the board, and envision himself at the point after he has already broken it. The blow itself must be imagined as already having split the board into two and passing right through it. Like other experiences in life, the first time is the hardest, because the body and mind are not certain that they can succeed. After you've broken your first board, you already know that you can do it.

What does board breaking have to do with the art of asking for a donation? They have a lot in common. It's much more relaxing to sit for an hour with a potential donor and chat about all sorts of things, exchange opinions, eat a meal together, and in the end part as friends – without asking for anything. Asking for a donation isn't exactly like a sale. A salesperson offers the potential buyer something in exchange and has to convince the buyer that the purchase is worthwhile. What physical item is a fundraiser selling to the donor? What is given in return for the donation?

I've often heard from senior executives in the business world about the sense of emptiness that accompanies their work, which focuses on the bottom line of their monetary profits. "I want to do something good. Something for the soul. To feel that I am contributing to society and helping others," many CEOs say.

My friend Larry Smith from Boston, a successful businessman, generous philanthropist, and former basketball player, told me one day during breakfast as we were enjoying the gorgeous colors of the New England autumn: "When I donated money to renovate and maintain the basketball courts in my hometown in Florida, I told the manager of the basketball team that I envy him. My work involves selling auto insurance policies, which isn't very exciting. You, I said to him, work in basketball training, teaching teens. Now that's what I call exciting!"

I heard this important lesson from a colleague who perfectly expressed what's so unique about fundraising work: "You need to think and feel like you are the one doing the donor a favor, and not the other way around. You are enabling the donor to do something virtuous and important with his or her money. Most donors are busy people, and it's difficult for them to make time for charity work. You're giving them the opportunity to do good and feel good about it."

In meetings with potential donors and partners in Israel and around the world, the fundraiser has a golden opportunity to get to know fascinating people. They are business leaders of international stature who can inspire us and teach us important lessons. We can learn to respect and even love them – as I did with D.

D. is one of the special people I had the privilege of meeting during my years of work in the resource development field. D. is an African American who was born in a small town in the United States. He was the only teen of color in an all-white school in the 1960s, at a time when African Americans were routinely treated like second-class citizens. D. went on to found a technology company. At first, it almost went bankrupt, but D. turned it into a great success. D. is a devoted Christian with a high regard for Israel and the Jewish people.

Although he is a sought-after and respected businessman and philanthropist, D. is constantly aware of his origins and takes advantage of any opportunity to share his wealth and wisdom with others. Every meeting with him is a source of inspiration for me. At lunch in his hometown, he shared with me this beautiful motto: "I don't work to make a living – I work to make a giving."

THE APPROACH: BOXING OR AIKIDO?

Boxing is characterized by aggressive combat. Force versus force, power versus power. Mutual bloodshed and head-on blows. The martial art of aikido (loosely translated from Japanese as "way of unifying energy"), on the other hand, is characterized by gentleness, circular movements, and elegance. A skilled aikido fighter does not apply his own strength against his opponent's strength, but instead feels his opponent's strength, merges with it, and takes advantage of it for his own benefit. There is great value to using the principles of aikido in fundraising, and the following sentence expresses this well: "The best donation is the donation given without a request." A good donation is one that makes the donor happy, given with exhilaration, willingly and with enthusiasm, not by force or arm-twisting.

I was once at a meeting where the head of a big educational organization put extreme pressure on a leading Israeli businessman, who was not exactly in prime health at the time, to make a large donation to his organization. His aggressive style was similar to that of a boxer: demand, application of pressure, immovability. It was very uncomfortable in that room; at the end of the meeting, no donation was given, and the donor left feeling frustrated and sour.

Here's another example of an aggressive, rude donation request. Every year at the end of the mournful fast day of Tisha b'Av, the people of Hoshaya stand outside the synagogue waiting for Maariv (the evening prayer service) to begin. Also standing outside is a man from a certain charity organization who comes to Hoshaya every year to ask for donations, since the final hours of a day of fasting and lamentation are certainly a prime time to give charity. His technique is composed of a fiery speech during the break between afternoon and evening prayers, followed by rounds in the synagogue courtyard, individual conversations with the people, and entreaties to open their hearts and their wallets.

I was standing with a group of people outside the synagogue when the fundraiser approached us. "Charity?" he urged. One of the people took out his wallet and handed him a fifty-shekel bill. "All the best," the donor said. The collector looked at the bill, then directed his harsh stare at the donor and replied: "Give another ten shekels! Make it sixty." The donor refused. The collector pushed. The donor again refused, and the collector walked away holding the fifty, leaving both of them – donor and collector – feeling frustrated and angry.

This doesn't mean that fundraisers should not be persistent and dedicated to their cause or that they shouldn't set a high bar for donations and pursue commitments unrelentingly. These elements are not only necessary but even expected of fundraisers. But they can be done the right way, pleasantly, with sensitivity toward the donor, his character, his needs, and his situation. They should always be accompanied by a smile and words of gratitude.

How to Ask?

You can always ask for a donation simply and directly, by saying, "I would like to invite you to make a donation of $X for our important project." But you can also find more creative, unique ways of asking, which are hard for donors to refuse and make them feel happy to oblige.

I once met with one of my major non-Jewish donors in the United States a few days before Passover, after the donor had already donated significant sums and even recruited a few of his friends to donate to my organization. I planned on asking him for another substantial sum and contemplated how I should go about asking. The night before the meeting, I held the gift that I had brought from Israel for him in my hands – a Passover Haggadah in English written by Rabbi Yisrael Meir Lau. I wanted to write him a nice dedication at the beginning of the book. Then a great idea hit me for how to ask for the donation.

The next day, during our meeting in his spacious office, after the chatting, pleasantries, and reports, I took Rabbi Lau's beautiful Haggadah out of my briefcase and moved to sit next to the donor. "Look at this," I began. "The Haggadah, which tells the story of the Jewish people's exodus from Egypt, includes a song called 'Dayenu.'" I explained to him what the word *dayenu* means ("it would have been enough") and what the Jews are thanking God for after leaving Egypt. "We say *dayenu* to you too," I continued. "If you had only donated to us yourself, it would have been enough. If you had donated to us and recruited some of your friends to donate even more, it would have been enough. And now, I would like to add another line to our 'Dayenu' song – and invite you to donate to our new project…"

The donor was so happy and amused with the way that I requested the donation that he didn't hesitate and agreed on the spot to donate for the third *dayenu*.

When to Ask?

I had a hard time finding the right time to ask an Israeli donor living in the United States for a donation. For a few years, I kept missing the window of opportunity. When I saw him in November or December, he told me that his donation budget for this year was already spent and that there was nothing left in the family fund. When I visited him in January or February, he apologized and said that the decision on how to distribute the funds for the year had not yet been made.

A different donor in the United States was a longtime friend. Unfortunately, he contracted a chronic illness, and his health slowly began to deteriorate. When I came to visit him, I felt that it was inappropriate to ask for a donation when he was dealing with such a big medical challenge. I decided that I would be better off not asking at all. But just a short time after I left his house, he called my cell phone and said in a tremulous voice, "You forgot something. You forgot to ask me for a donation!" The gesture touched me so much that I didn't even care about the amount of his donation.

Where to Ask?

At home or at the office, at a restaurant or in the garden, in the car or at the airport? Of course, you often can't dictate the location for the meeting with your potential donor, since he's usually the one who decides. Nevertheless, one should be aware of and sensitive to the location element. During one of my fundraising campaigns, I was staying in New York with a colleague. We tried to meet with a certain wealthy personality in the city to ask for a donation for our organization. The meeting was scheduled, and we spent a long time preparing for it, learning about the donor and his interests, planning what to say, what to ask for, who would ask, etc. Just an hour before the meeting, the donor's secretary called us. "His plans for today have changed. He isn't feeling well and is on the way to the hospital for an urgent, invasive test. The only time I have in his meeting schedule for today is a twenty-minute window after the test at the hospital. Should I write you down?" We exchanged glances and then declined the secretary's offer, sending our wishes for good health. It wasn't an appropriate time to meet with the donor.

PREPARATION FOR THE ASK

Before a meeting during which you plan to ask for a donation, you must prepare several things. The following is a checklist that you should review before every meeting with a donor:

1. **Project proposals.** Despite today's advanced technological options and the ability to show a donor a proposal on an iPad, present it with a mobile projector, and/or email it, it is still important to leave well-written and tastefully designed professional hard-copy material in the donor's hand. This will allow donors to take a second look and be impressed with what you are offering as well as to have something to pass on to other family members who may have input into deciding on family gifts.

2. **Donor history.** Be sure to check information about the donor's prior donations to the organization, if any. It is important to update longtime donors about how past donations have been utilized. Bring stories, letters, anecdotes, and real-life examples of the good things that they have already facilitated with their donations. It is also important to be very familiar with the amounts of a donor's past donations. Donors will often ask, "How much did I give you last year?" Inability to answer this question will embarrass any fundraiser. It is also important to be able to say something like the following to the donor: "Over the past two years, you donated $20,000 to us each year. I understand that your business was blessed and has grown this year. Can you share some of that blessing with our organization and increase your contribution this year?"

3. **Multiple donation options.** I once met with a British donor and asked him for a donation for a certain project. "That project does not interest me at all!" he said to me decisively. "But I want to help you. If you can

offer me a different project, I would be happy to consider it." Luckily, I had another proposal for a different project in my briefcase, and the donor was pleased with it. In this way, the opportunity to receive his donation was not lost.

4. **Facts about the donor.** Do your homework and get updated information about the donor, his or her businesses, family, and interests. It would be very embarrassing to enter a meeting with a donor and discover only during the course of the meeting that his wife died suddenly just two months earlier. Or on the flip side, the fundraiser will get extra credit points for congratulating the donor during their meeting when the football team she owns wins the championship, when his daughter graduates medical school, when she is granted an honorary degree, or even on his recent wedding anniversary. Up-to-date information can be found with some diligence, and the ability to use it wisely and at the right time is extremely critical.

Gathering, Using, and Storing Information

The importance of accurate, specific information about donors and their donations cannot be overstated. When I attempted to try to receive a donation from a Canadian billionaire, I decided to learn more about him, his family, his values, his giving history, the people usually surrounding him, and his financial abilities. I was able to find out through the internet that the donor's wealth was estimated at $4 billion. I also was told by a friend who lives in his city that a decade ago, a representative of a large Israeli organization also used to live in the same city and had succeeded in receiving a donation of a million dollars from him.

I found that fortunate fundraiser and took him for lunch, and he shared with me a vast amount of information that I would never have learned through electronic sources. Among other things, I learned about the donor's interests, the best way to approach him, which of his family members are involved in donation decisions, and more. Equipped with this detailed information, I flew fifteen hours to meet with the donor's daughter. Sitting across from her, I felt like I had known her for years. The information I had was so precise that at some point in the conversation, I felt she was just verifying what I already knew. That specific meeting did not end with a donation commitment (to my disappointment), but it was the beginning of a new and potentially fruitful relationship.

The information is of course vital for the first meeting with a donor (after all, you can only make a first impression once), but it's necessary for the rest of the relationship too. I once met with a potential donor for lunch and was planning to ask him for a donation for the first time. Imagine how embarrassed I felt when I found out that his father had passed away just a month earlier, and I had no idea. My embarrassment was twofold: I hadn't come to comfort him after his father died, and I had also asked him for a donation at an inappropriate time. Or, in another situation, I went to ask a donor in the United States for a donation just two days after his company's stock fell by several dozen percent. We all learn the hard way!

Where is the information? Information about donors can be found in many places. There are internet search engines, the newspapers, literature about foundations (most of which is online today too), and websites with research and information designated specifically for the nonprofit sector such as GuideStar. There are lists of wealthy people and donors, such as *Fortune* magazine lists. Company websites often feature the biographies of their senior executives, and organizations describe the members of their boards of directors. Of course, we can't forget the old, classic sources of information – people. There's often nothing that can top a telephone call to a colleague or friend, or a coffee date to learn and prepare for a meeting with a potential donor.

Sift the wheat from the chaff. Today, the challenge is not finding information, but sifting through the information to find the important parts in the ocean of information available in the palm of any person connected to the internet. Which parts are important to us? Which sources of information are reliable? What is the agenda of the person publishing the information? When a person types the name "Oprah Winfrey" into Google's search engine, over twenty-eight million results will appear. The first pages on the search engine list are pages from the internet encyclopedia Wikipedia; from television shows posted on YouTube; and from the official websites of initiatives, companies, and foundations founded and owned by Oprah. This order is no coincidence, of course.

The search engine optimization (SEO) industry, or in simpler terms, "the stuff I put on my website so that the world first sees the content that I want it to see and am paying for it to see," is a professional and expensive industry. For this reason, especially when famous people are involved, it is worth skipping to pages 20 and 30 and checking what else the search has to offer. It's a good idea to become familiar with a few trustworthy information sources and concentrate on them when searching for information, at least at the first stage of your search. A US-based organization called the Foundation Center maintains one of the most comprehensive databases on US foundations and increasingly more international foundations.

You may also want to check leading international and local financial journals and less sensational newspapers, since they may be more reliable in their reporting on wealthy personalities and more careful about reporting baseless rumors. Professional networks such as LinkedIn offer information that people have published about themselves. Again – whenever it's possible to speak to acquaintances who are familiar with the person and can give you updated, personal information, try to do so.

Using information. I raised my first million-dollar gift in New Orleans. I traveled there with the late Itzik Shavit from the Israel Education Fund in order to present a new library project at Tel Hai College to the Woldenberg Foundation. This is a family foundation that amassed its wealth primarily from the alcoholic beverage business. Before the flight and the critical presentation to the board members of the foundation, I tried to collect every possible piece of information about the foundation and its board. I managed to find a picture of one of the prominent members who was formerly a basketball player. For the sake of this story, I'll call him Jacob. I memorized the information that I found in order to integrate messages into my presentation that would appeal to my audience.

When Itzik and I arrived at the foundation's offices, situated in the impressive historical building that housed the family company, the receptionist asked us to wait in the conference room, which was lined from wall to wall with various types of alcoholic beverages. In the meantime, I visited the restroom, and when I opened the door to the stall, I was shocked to see Jacob himself standing right in front of me, inside the stall. I managed to recover my senses a few seconds later and only then realized that it wasn't the real Jacob, but rather a life-sized picture of him, in basketball uniform, on the door of the stall. A short time later, standing opposite Jacob and his fellow administrators, as I presented the library project and our donation request of one million dollars, I already felt as if Jacob and I knew each other almost intimately.

I arrived at a different meeting with a donor in the United States after practically memorizing his autobiography. Until this very day, I am unsure whether he noticed that I was quoting lines from his book during our conversation, or whether the messages and values that I presented were just exceptionally similar to the messages in his book. What I do know is that the meeting ended with a sizable donation and the development of a new friendship.

Ensure your information is up-to-date. It is important to remember that we live in a dynamic world, and something published last year may not be relevant anymore. It would be pretty embarrassing to ask a donor how his wife is doing and then discover that they got divorced two years ago, or ask a donor about her son and then hear that he recently died of a severe illness. You wouldn't want to ask a donor for a large donation and then realize too late that he's in the process of filing for bankruptcy. Before any meeting or contact with a donor, it's critical to refresh your sources to verify all information. When in doubt, it's usually better to remain silent instead of chatter and say nonsense.

Use information sensitively and ethically. At one of the organizations where I managed the fundraising efforts, there was an internal audit that focused, among other topics, on fundraising operations. The auditor did a thorough job and checked donation lists, work plans, summaries of overseas trips, invoices, and reports of expenses. I met with the auditor several times during the process. At our very first meeting, he asked for information about the organization's donors. I refused to provide it. I explained to him that some of the information is personal and classified, and even the president of the organization doesn't see it, because these are things that people told me and didn't intend for me to share.

When he finally submitted his report to the organization's audit committee, the committee asked for my response. I told them the same thing about the importance of discretion and even added that it was also in the organization's best interest for as few eyes as possible to peruse its donor information. The audit committee accepted my position and approved for me to continue to keep the information classified. When a fundraising professional develops relationships and sometimes even friendships with wealthy, influential people, this also comes with a serious responsibility to apply discretion and sensitivity.

Get a donor relations management (DRM) system. Similar to a customer relations management system (CRM), which is better known, the role of this system is to collect, manage, maintain, and improve information about donors and donations. There are various types of systems, free of charge or off the shelf, and there are even custom-designed systems to address an organization's specific needs. Using such a system is even more relevant for large organizations with many donors in a range of countries, as well as a broad donation history.

The program enables the fundraising manager and the organization's management to do many things: track a donor's donation history, track receipt of donations, track fundraising successes in comparison with the goals on their work plan, send a request to a donor asking for an annual contribution, track multiyear donations, produce management reports, send birthday greetings to donors, and more. Purchasing, tailor-making, updating, and using such a system involves an investment of time and money. Not every organization needs a DRM. An organization taking its first steps in the fundraising world with just twenty-two donors can get along just fine with simple Excel spreadsheets.

How Much to Request?

I once met with a donor in New York. Knowing that he was Chairman of the Board of Governors of one of the largest universities in Israel, I figured my chances of receiving a donation from him for the academic institution that I was representing were pretty negligible, as it was even considered one of his institution's competitors. Because our meeting happened to be on my birthday, I told the donor, "I know that you're the chairman of a different institution, but in honor of my birthday, I'd like to invite you to donate to my organization." "How much do you want?" he asked. I mentioned a sum of a few thousand dollars, and he immediately took out his checkbook and wrote out a donation. I thanked him from the bottom of my heart but at the same time, I wondered whether I had asked for too little.

About six months later, I met with the same donor again. At some point during our conversation, he asked me, "Tell me, did I donate to you already?" "Yes," I replied. "How much did I give?" he asked. I told him the amount. "That's too little!" he exclaimed. "Talk to me at the beginning of the calendar year about a bigger donation." And I did, and his next donation was about ten times larger than the first one.

So how much should you ask for? That's one of the "million-dollar questions" in fundraising. It's not easy to answer, but there are a few rules of thumb regarding what you should be checking:

- An estimate of the donor's wealth and charitable giving capacity.
- Information about the donor's gifts to other organizations throughout the years and especially in recent years.
- History of the donor's gifts to your organization. How much and for what projects?
- The financial situation of the donor, of his or her company, and the industry as a whole. Remember that economics and psychology go hand in hand.
- Gut feeling. My friend Peter Rzepka escaped from war-ravaged Europe, survived a stint in Siberia, and finally made it to America the long way, to establish a thriving family and family business together with his wife Aliki. Peter once told me, "Trust your gut feeling. It's more often right than wrong." This piece of life advice, which he learned under extreme duress, has tremendous value.
- It's better to ask for a bit too much than to ask for too little. If the answer is a flat-out no, the amount you asked for doesn't matter anyway. If the answer is positive, the worst thing that can happen is that you'll get less than you asked for.

In the end, it's very hard to know how much to ask for, as the following story demonstrates. A few years ago, one of the heads of the Israeli intelligence services met with representatives from one of the wealthy Persian Gulf states.

The topic of the meeting was unofficial cooperation against Iran's nuclear program. The Israeli representative answered the questions of the Arab state's representatives by explaining various possible methods of operation to respond to the Iranian nuclear problem, all developed in Israel. "But development of these means is very expensive and requires large sums of money," the Israeli said. "How much do you need in order to do it?" the senior Arab official inquired. The Israeli didn't know exactly how much it would cost, but he felt obligated to answer, so he rounded up the figures and told them it would cost $3 billion. The Arab group began to chuckle. The Israeli thought he had exaggerated in his estimate and asked them why they were laughing. "That's all?! That's all you need?! That's small change!"

Creating an Appropriate Atmosphere

Donation requests are received by potential donors with more of an open heart when made in an appropriate atmosphere, which will also be more pleasant for the fundraiser. I once traveled to Canada to meet with a major foundation executive. Based on the homework I did before the trip, I understood that the manager was not a very easygoing woman and didn't make friends easily, and that it would be hard to penetrate her steel armor. At the same time, I also learned that without the support of this foundation manager, there was no chance of advancing toward a possible donation.

I arrived at her office for the meeting on a frigid day, exhausted after a series of long flights from Israel to Canada. The foundation executive led me from the lavish lobby to her office, with a cold expression that warned that she was a very busy woman who didn't have much time to dedicate to the likes of me. When I sat on the chair in her office, I noticed a huge sword hanging on the wall and realized this was my chance to break the ice. I asked her about the sword. Her face lit up, and she began to tell me a long story about the origins of the sword and her fondness for weapons. When she took a break to breathe, I mentioned that I do karate. The conversation flowed as we discussed martial arts, and the atmosphere was relaxed and friendly. At this point, we were meant to discuss the possibility of donating to my organization and whether its activities suited the foundation's objectives. But in terms of setting the atmosphere, I had nothing to worry about.

FOLLOW-UP AFTER THE ASK
What if the Donor Agrees?

An experienced fundraiser is used to hearing "no" more often than "yes." The rule is, "If you hear yes twice for every ten times you hear no, your situation is good." So what should a fundraiser do when she hears the long-awaited yes?

- Shake the donor's hand in gratitude and appreciation, and look her straight in the eye. The handshake symbolizes several things: confirmation of the promise to donate and reinforcement with a handshake. It also expresses your thanks that the donor decided to give. In addition, it removes any doubt that the answer was really yes. It has happened that I heard a positive answer from a donor and he remembered something different later.

- Write a follow-up letter. A few days after receiving a donation promise, it's a good idea to write a thank-you letter that includes the donation details and what the money is earmarked for, as well as the amount, the date that it will be transferred, details for sending the donation, etc.

- If possible and if customary in the organization, prepare an agreement between the donor and the receiving organization. Sometimes a simple letter confirming the donation is sufficient, but for large donations or complicated agreements that span several years, considering the fact that people working at organizations change and none of us are immortal, such an agreement is important and valuable, in order to coordinate expectations, schedules, and other details.

- Make a plan to cultivate the donor, leverage her donation to obtain other donors, and maintain contact with the donor and her family to update on the progress or promise.

What if the Answer Is No?

It's always a good idea to listen to the donor with a smile and empathy, even when the answer to your donation request is negative. I once sat with one of the wealthy members of a Jewish community in the United States, whose wealth is estimated at several billion dollars. After a captivating conversation about Israel, security issues, and Jewish identity, we arrived at the reason for my visit, and I asked for a donation. The billionaire looked at me warmly and told me that he was already committed to different organizations in Israel and therefore could not contribute to mine.

Inside, I thought, "With all his money, after being in touch for many years and all these meetings with him, can't he give me anything at all?" But on the outside, I listened politely, nodded my head, smiled pleasantly, and answered in an understanding tone. Never cause a donor to feel embarrassed or unpleasant. Nothing good will come out of it. You won't get a significant donation (except for maybe a few crumbs to make you go away), and you'll hurt the feelings of a person who doesn't actually owe you or your organization anything at all.

Moreover, life is cyclical. He said no today, but his opinion and/or abilities could change tomorrow, or you might be representing a different cause that speaks to him more. Always leave a pleasant feeling wherever you go, characterized by respect and appreciation. After the meeting and the frustrating response that you received, don't be lazy – send that donor who didn't give anything a nice thank-you letter. Thank him for giving you his time, listening to you, and showing interest in the cause that you represent. Ask for an opportunity to meet him again, and invite him to visit you when he's in the area.

Sometimes, no simply means "not now." When I called my good friend Bill in the United States and asked to meet with him during my upcoming visit to his city, he clarified that he would be happy to see me but that he couldn't donate at the moment, due to a slow period in his business. Bill is a generous donor and had given significant sums in the past to projects that I promoted. His answer was not only in response to my question about a possible meeting, but also a test of my friendship. Had I failed the test, that definitely would have been the end of our relationship and the possibility that he would ever donate to me in the future. "Of course I'd be happy to see you," I replied, and we did meet. While he couldn't donate anything that year, financial situations change, and later, he donated again.

When Does Maybe Mean No?

I met with George just a few times. Whenever I was in his city in North America, I would try to see him. George is a businessman with ideological and religious ties to Israel, and he even owns a few businesses located in Israel. After our first two meetings, which were dedicated to introductions and building a relationship, I asked him to donate to my organization. His answer was ambivalent. It sounded something like this: "I plan on donating at some point but not right now, and it also depends on my wife." I received the same type of answer from him two more times over the next two years.

George is always happy to meet with me, talk to me about grand affairs, and hear about what's going on in Israel; he has even used the connection with me once or twice to get in touch with key personalities in Israel. He always asked me good, specific questions about the organization I was working for, its budget, its areas of operation and specialties, but I never got a donation from him, not even a small one.

At some point, I decided that George's maybe was actually a no, and that I was apparently wasting my time (and his). I stopped scheduling meetings with him and asking for donations, although I did keep in touch with him as an acquaintance. This is not an easy decision. There are many cases in which a potential donor will say straight out, "I won't donate to your organization." This type of response may be caused by several factors, such as a lack of interest in the organization's activity, an unsuccessful history with the organization or its leadership, a focus on different projects and areas of interest, and more – and all this is legitimate. But what do you do when the situation is not black and white? There are a few options. You can continue trying, at least for a while longer. You can decrease the intensity of the connection, such as keeping in touch only by phone and correspondence, without pursuing distant, expensive meetings. Or, you can stop viewing the person as a potential donor altogether.

Coordinating Expectations

A Chabad rabbi who built a Chabad center in one of the secular communities in northern Israel told me the following story. When he asked to meet with me to hear my advice on fundraising for his activities, I happily obliged, but I mentioned that Chabad is considered the best fundraising organization in the world, and I probably have more to learn from them than I can offer. Here's his story:

> A few years ago, I traveled to Florida and stayed with friends, hoping to raise donations for projects that I was initiating for Chabad's operations. After I spoke at a synagogue, an elegantly dressed man wearing a

three-piece suit, with gold cufflinks on his white shirt, approached me
and thanked me sincerely for the wonderful speech. "I would be happy
to host you tomorrow at my office," the impressive man said to me.

I figured that this was an opportunity sent to me from heaven to
collect a donation, and I scheduled a meeting for the next day. When
I entered his fancy office, I noticed that there was no mezuzah in his
doorway. We sat for a long time talking about faith, God, charity, and
family. The man thanked me for the captivating conversation and
promised to send me a donation by mail. When I returned to Israel,
I was very optimistic and believed that this wealthy man from Florida
would be providing the salvation I needed. The day after I came back
to Israel, I went to a Judaica store and bought him a pretty mezuzah
cover and an expensive scroll to put inside. I invested several hundred
shekels in that purchase from a budget I didn't even have, as an investment in the big donor that God sent me. Two weeks later, I received an
envelope in the mail from the affluent man in Florida. Hands shaking
in anticipation, I opened the envelope, and inside, I found a polite letter and a twenty-dollar bill!

GEARING UP TO DO IT AGAIN
Olympic Champions Practice Too
Practice and polish your skills. Don't hesitate and don't spare resources and
time when planning a big donation request. After the 2006 Second Lebanon
War and the international attention that the Galilee region received due to the
missile attacks by Hizballah, we at Tel Hai College experienced an unprecedented level of attention. One of the organizations that we forged a long-
term strategic partnership with is the United Jewish Israel Appeal (UJIA) of
Great Britain. After a period of initial examination and introductions, a delegation of leaders of the British Jewish community and some of its wealthiest
members were scheduled to arrive for a visit. The honorable representatives
planned to come to the Upper Galilee in three helicopters.

This visit had major potential for significant donations to the college, and
especially for construction of the new campus that we were building at the
time. To maximize the impact of the gorgeous landscape around the campus, with snow-capped Mount Hermon glistening like a diamond on top of a

golden ring, we erected a special event tent on a hill overlooking the construction site, where we could host our guests. I was given the task of delivering our
message. The college's CEO and I spent hours polishing our message so we
could deliver it in the most optimal manner, and in just eight minutes.

Because I understood the importance of the event and the need for serious
preparation, I practiced with a senior communications coach who specializes
in body language and getting the message across. I practiced those eight minutes again and again, and the visit was indeed a great success. The message
was clear, and the donations came in. UJIA became the college's most important donor and contributed many millions over the years. Once again, I realized the truth of the sentence I often repeated to my karate students practicing
for their black belt test: "I never met a karateka who regretted practicing too
much for the black belt test."

Excite Yourself

In order to impress and excite donors, a fundraiser must be capable of motivating herself and feeling excitement about her organization's activities and
accomplishments. When Vera Muravitz does this, it's an art. Vera, Bar-Ilan
University's legendary fundraiser, told me that before asking for large donations, she takes a walk on the beach next to her home in Netanya and practices
the main messages that she plans on delivering to the donor. "Sometimes,
when I walk on the promenade along the beach, I get so engrossed in the
details of the story that I'm planning to tell that I forget I'm just practicing. I
feel so moved by my own story that I start shedding emotional tears myself."
Fundraisers who don't feel moved by their own stories (at least some of them)
are missing something. Excitement is contagious. Enthusiasm gets others
involved. Words are not enough to convince someone.

Above All, Remember Why

Alan Gill, Executive Vice President Emeritus of the American Jewish Joint
Distribution Committee (JDC), views fundraising meetings as sacred
moments:

> At fundraising meetings, I remember and concentrate on the fact that
> I'm representing people who can't be in the room themselves, people

who need me to help them as the go-between connecting them with the donor. I represent them – their fears, their needs. When I ask for a donation, I feel like an emissary for a sacred mission. I feel that the meeting between myself and the donor is almost a holy event. It focuses on the person and his soul, on the things that are truly important to him. It highlights the meaning of his life and how he succeeds in realizing this meaning by helping others.

ETHICS IN FUNDRAISING
Is It OK to Take Any Donation?

This is a loaded question and a central part of the fundraising world, and I will not go into it in depth here. Quite a few of the big philanthropists in the world, and in the Jewish world as well, amassed their great wealth in ways that were not always on the right side of the law. There are those who claim that taking donations from a donor whose money originated from an old sin helps cleanse the sins of those ancestors. There are those who say that it's none of the recipient's business – if it's legal, it doesn't matter if it reeks a bit. There are those who completely ignore the entire issue so they won't have to deal with it. Assuming that the donation must comply with the laws of the country, the rest is up to the discretion of the leaders of the organization.

When I managed the fundraising team of one of the leading academic institutions in the north, an oligarch of Russian origin became famous for giving sizable donations to almost anyone who asked him. The CEO urged me to contact that oligarch and ask for a donation, but I refused. Rumors were spreading at the time about the questionable sources of his wealth, and they were compounded by the unpleasant feeling I had, based on a random encounter with him at a conference. "Our fundraising efforts are succeeding nicely without him. Let's not ruin our good reputation and our luck with a donor like him," I demurred. Indeed, a few years later, the rumors became known facts, and everyone at the organization was happy that we hadn't had anything to do with him.

There are donations that an organization must not take. For example, an American donor called me and asked to make a donation to the academic institution as a scholarship for his relative, who was studying at the school at the time. Despite my regret over losing the donation, I had to explain to him that we were not allowed to take a donation and give tax-deductible credit for it if the donation was earmarked for the man's relative. He should be giving the money directly to his relative, without receiving the tax credit for the donation.

Look Out for the Donor's Interests

A donor who contributes to an organization becomes a kind of partner. Not every donor feels that way. But many organization directors are not interested in more partners who will give them advice and ask questions. The size of the donation does not always correspond to the level of involvement and sense of partnership that the donor feels. Sometimes, a donor who gives a modest contribution actually gets deeply involved. But in principle, the expression "be our partner," so often used by fundraisers, should be an obligation, not just lip service and a euphemism for talking about money.

Who is responsible for taking care of these "partners" properly? The fundraiser, of course. Serious pressure was once put on me by management to approve using donation money for a different purpose than what the donor had intended. I adamantly refused. I told them that the responsibility toward this donor, whom only I knew personally, was mine alone. The donor contributed for a specific cause and relied on us to invest his donation in that cause. I said that because he wasn't here with us and hadn't even demanded that we send him detailed reports signed by our attorneys and accountants, we were obligated to be twice as careful about our ethics and trustworthiness. To the management, such a donor is often just a name and a source of funds. The fundraiser is the one who usually meets with the donor, works his or her magic, makes commitments, keeps in touch, and praises the cause that the donation will support. Thus, the fundraiser is also the one responsible for preserving the donor's interests as a partner in the organization.

Bolster Your Credibility

Over the past years, awareness has increased worldwide of the need for an objective stamp of credibility for nonprofit organizations. In the past, responsibility for confirming that a nonprofit is managed according to the law and within required parameters fell on the NGO's shoulders. But unfortunately, there were many cases of officially approved organizations whose actual dealings were not very proper at all. Today, organizations such as GuideStar and Charity Navigator offer potential donors or partners extensive, reliable information regarding the organization's conduct and effectivity. Scores such as "ranking of the organization's effectivity level" are becoming market standards.

Donors, companies, and foundations regularly demand this data about nonprofits before making their decisions regarding donations, parallel to stars for hotels or Michelin restaurant ratings. Make sure your organization conducts itself in such a way as to rank well. If a given deal, accounting method, or any other organizational action won't smell good to potential and existing donors, just don't do it!

CHAPTER 4

PREPARING A FUNDRAISING WORK PLAN

In fundraising, focusing, prioritizing, and sifting the wheat from the chaff are vitally important.

The late General Israel Tal was a division commander on the southern front when the 1967 Six-Day War broke out. General Tal stood before his soldiers and briefed them before going to battle. He concluded with the following message: "These are the orders and the battle plans, but in war, the events never go according to plan. Be aware that as soon as the shooting begins, everything will change. Remember the main tasks and aim to complete them at all costs."

While fundraising isn't a war (though perhaps some fundraisers will disagree with me on that), we too must combine our plans (work plan) with the appropriate actions and improvisations to adapt to the changing reality, while keeping our primary goals in mind. The work plan is our road map, our compass. It allows us to present plans to the management, justify required budgets, plan personnel and tasks, and set fundraising goals. A fundraising work plan does not need to be very detailed, but it does need to be focused, realistic, ambitious, and clear.

ESTABLISHING WORK METHODS

A fundraising work plan (annual or biannual) often includes the following:

1. Primary objectives of the organization's fundraising system
2. Setting specific objectives for the fundraising operations

3. Analysis of strengths, weaknesses, opportunities, and threats (SWOT) related to the organization's fundraising efforts
4. List of donation possibilities (fundraising projects) according to areas and priorities
5. Analysis and plan for fundraising activities in different locations throughout the world
6. List of main donors and plan for retaining them
7. Plan for donor recruitment, appreciation, and development
8. Plan for developing volunteer leadership
9. Promoting an organization-wide atmosphere of fundraising
10. Plan for preparing and distributing marketing materials, and organizational branding
11. Plan for recruiting, training, and managing fundraising personnel
12. Indices and criteria to evaluate success

When preparing work plans, and especially when setting quantitative fundraising goals (total annual donations, total number of donors, number of new donors, etc.), it's important to carefully navigate between two extremes. One is the desire to raise the bar, fundraise more, set fundraising records, make the management happy, show some competitive spirit, and various other motives that will push the goal higher. The second is the need to set a goal that can actually be met, that is logical in light of the organization's resources (personnel, budget, existing infrastructure, economic atmosphere, donations in previous years), and that will leave room for growth in future years. A realistic fundraising goal must take all of these elements into account, remembering the saying "Man plans and God laughs."

Combining Office Work with Field Work

For most people, it's not easy or natural and can even be embarrassing to look the person sitting opposite you straight in the eye and ask for a donation. It's a lot easier and more pleasant to sit in front of your computer, in an air-conditioned office, and send letters, donation requests, and information pamphlets. Office work is certainly a part of fundraising; preparing materials, updates, marketing brochures, and video clips; organizing events; and operating the website are all important tasks. But combining them with direct, face-to-face contact with donors is what fundraising is all about. The balance between these two aspects depends on the working style of the fund-raiser, the personnel, the type of organization being represented, and the scope of the contacts.

Preparing an Annual Fundraising Budget

Like any of an organization's activities, its fundraising operations should have a designated budget. It's best for the budget to be part of the overall budget of the organization, and not based on percentages of the anticipated donations. Although it is sometimes difficult to set aside a new budget to finance fundraising efforts, the decision to rely on existing or future donations is doomed for failure. This budget should include the range of operations that will be necessary for fundraising, including salaries, free-lancer payments, marketing content, design, printing of materials, website construction and maintenance, events, conference attendance, travel and accommodations overseas, and more. It is always important to leave some room in the budget for unplanned activity, since the best things happen when you least expect them…

Seizing Opportunities

One morning, I received an email from one of the donors to an organization where I managed fundraising. He had attached an invitation from a foundation I'd never heard of to submit a request for proposals (RFP). The foundation was welcoming requests between one and three million dollars. I tried to find more information about the foundation online but was unsuccessful. I called about ten of my colleagues – foundation managers and fundraisers. None of them had heard of the mysterious foundation. For a moment, I thought that it was a hoax, but then I reminded myself of the saying "Opportunity some-times knocks softly – you have to listen carefully."

I consulted with the president and the CEO, and together we decided to submit a proposal for funding for two capital projects. We weren't sure how much to request for each project. In the end, we decided to ask for one million dollars for one project and two million dollars for the other (those were the amounts that we had determined would be necessary in order to name the building after the donor). We began communicating with this foundation, which included preparing documents, answering questions, and scheduling an introductory visit. A few months later, the foundation's representatives arrived for a visit to our organization, which resulted in their contribution of two million dollars!

Kime

Kime is a Japanese term taken from the world of martial arts. Loosely translated, it means focusing the right strength at the right time and in the right place. In fundraising, focusing, prioritizing, and sifting the wheat from the chaff are vitally important. With experience, a fundraiser learns to develop tools and sensitivities that help differentiate, for example, between a potentially big donor and a donor who demands attention but will have a hard time contributing a significant sum. Or, sensing the difference between the guy who will connect you to other donors and the guy who boasts about his extensive connections, most of whom won't actually show up at the benefit event he organizes for you.

Kime will also help you decide when a trip overseas is justified and necessary, even for just one meeting with a single donor, and when the ten meetings you have arranged overseas aren't substantial enough to justify the time and monetary investment.

In fundraising work, there's always something to do. You can always make another phone call, send another email, set up another meeting, or do more research. *Kime* pushes you to sometimes just say "enough!" You need to rest, too, and leave something for tomorrow. Resting is power too.

INTERNATIONAL OR CROSS-COUNTRY TRAVEL

Many organization managers I have advised over the years on setting up a fundraising system have told me during our very first meeting that they strive to raise money in wealthy international cities. "I would like to organize a dinner in New York...," "I heard that X organization raised a lot of money in London...," "I know someone in Singapore who told me that he knows rich people..." What I usually do is smile and suggest that they start their fundraising activities locally, ideally in the area where their organization is active. I say, "Wait, have you already fundraised in wealthy local neighborhoods in the vicinity?"

On a more serious note, fundraising cross-country or overseas means investing money in travel costs and accommodations as well as a time investment. You must know the language and understand the culture, and you need connections. In addition, you will need to do long-distance follow-up.

Therefore, not every person or organization should immediately turn to long-distance or overseas sources to raise donations. Begin in town or in state. Moreover, potential donors overseas will often ask the fundraiser or organization manager: "Do you have local donors? How much do they donate?" The fundraiser will be more confident when hearing this question and similar ones if able to respond, "Of course, we have received donations from generous local sources, including companies, private donors, and members of our board of directors."

To Travel or Not to Travel?

When is it worth traveling internationally or cross-country? Fundraising is not an exact science. Sometimes, you'll embark on a fundraising trip overseas after preparing and practicing, with the best materials in your briefcase and with backing from local donors and prescheduled meetings that look promising – but you'll still come home empty-handed. In contrast, sometimes those who aren't as prepared have good luck, and one successful meeting, even an unplanned one, can change everything for the better. However, nothing can replace good preparation, and fate is usually on the side of those who look out for themselves. So when is it worth your while to travel? Consider the following conditions to check whether a fundraising trip cross-country or overseas is in order:

1. If traveling internationally, the organization is capable of receiving tax-exempt donations overseas independently, via an independent legal entity or a local Friends group that transfers the donation to your organization.
2. The organization has basic marketing materials in English or the relevant local language that describe the organization and its giving opportunities.
3. The organization is capable of initiating and coordinating a few meetings with potential donors who can either donate themselves or connect you to significant donors.

4. The organization is financially able to finance a cross-country or overseas trip.
5. The organization is capable of maintaining the connections developed during the trip – including repeat visits later.
6. All of these prerequisites are irrelevant in certain circumstances. If, for example, you received a phone call from a Canadian billionaire, who asked to meet you personally as soon as possible in order to hear about your organization and consider how to help you – forget everything you just read here about prerequisites, buy an airline ticket, and fly right over.

When shouldn't you travel long distances to fundraise? There are periods when it's not the best idea to plan a long-distance fundraising trip. During holidays and regular vacation periods, no matter what, people prefer to be with their families, not spend their time in meetings. Appointments with fundraisers are perceived by donors as part of their everyday work.

During periods of extreme weather, especially in the winter in Europe and North America, not only is it a possibility that bad weather will postpone all your meetings (because your plane can't land at its destination), but the whole trip is unpleasant. The truth is that anyone who can afford it prefers to migrate in the winter to warmer regions, such as Florida, Arizona, or Spain. For years, I traveled to fundraise in Sweden, where I enjoyed a great relationship with several individuals and communities. Only on one occasion were they willing to meet me when it wasn't springtime. I arrived in October, and even then, it was so cold that I understood why they prefer not to host people from the Middle East in the winter, regardless of how nice their hospitality is.

Where to Go –and What to Do When You Get There

Destination: opportunity. If you have a dedicated donor who is able to contribute significantly and is also a well-connected and respected member of his community, and he offers to host you in New York or London and invite a group of his friends to hear you – go right away. If you don't have this opportunity, then you will need to go where you can get your foot in the door. Find a potential friend, existing supporter, or contact person who could open up the first opportunities for you, and then decide where to start.

When I forged a good relationship with such a person in the United States, I identified his potential, the span of his influence, and his ability to connect others to his ideas, and I marked his city as a center for my fundraising activity. I traveled there a few times a year, gradually succeeding in recruiting more and more donors from that city.

I'm here – what now? First of all, it's a good idea to know what you're going to do long before you reach your destination. Before your flight – and sufficiently in advance, because Americans and Europeans don't like last-minute plans – you must prepare a trip itinerary. However, leave enough flexibility and time for new meetings to be scheduled during the visit, usually after someone you meet with offers to introduce you to another person. I am often asked, "How much longer are you going to be here? I would be happy to introduce you to X. Do you have any free time?"

Planning your trip itinerary. The trip should be planned in advance to give you enough time to make contact, coordinate, and prepare for meetings with people who are usually very busy. It's a good idea to arrange a few "anchor meetings" in the various areas that you plan to visit. I usually first schedule a meeting with the most important and central donor (or few donors) in that specific city. If I see that I will not be able to meet with him or her, I will consider deferring my visit to that city to a different time or even change the order of my visits to various locations in order to adapt myself to the important donor's availability.

After these fixed meetings are scheduled and the order of my visits to the various locations is coordinated, I can begin trying to schedule meetings with additional people: existing donors, potential donors with whom I've been in contact, new contacts introduced by friends in the city, and other people worth meeting. Always save time for friends, acquaintances, and colleagues who are not donors, but whom you will see to keep yourself up to date, collect information, and stay in touch.

Creating an itinerary for a fundraising trip is an art. You will gradually learn how to plan the timing and duration of each leg of the trip, determine the intervals between meetings, plan where and when to hold the meetings, establish their order, reschedule meetings to fit in more contacts (without offending anyone), and so on.

Learning the playing field. It is desirable, especially during your first visits to new locations, to learn as much as possible about the place and types of people. For example, when a fundraiser comes to Montreal, she should prepare her basic homework and know that there are two official languages there (English and French), that it is a country of immigrants and very large geographically but not densely populated, that it is very cold in the winter. She should know the names of the city's wealthy and the influential figures, and that the most popular sport in Canada is ice hockey (a Canadian donor once insisted on taking me to watch an ice hockey game, explaining that I could not possibly come to Canada to raise money without a minimal grasp of this sport).

Fundraisers traveling overseas should open a local newspaper and scan the headlines. Ten minutes of reading will give you important information that you can use in your meetings with local donors, such as the names of the leading sports teams, the state of the local economy, which scandals are in the news, and more. Wisely using this information during a meeting can earn you extra credit points and help you avoid embarrassing mistakes, too.

Cultivating Donors While Traveling

Why would donors want to see you? Y., a longtime, respected fundraiser, once shared with me his perspective on success when meeting a donor. "The most accurate definition of a successful result after a donor meeting is that the donor is willing to see you again. After all, during the meeting, not only did he give you his precious time, you even asked him for money at the end! If he's willing to meet again, you've succeeded."

So why indeed do donors want to meet fundraisers? The short answer comes from the list of reasons people donate money in general. The fundraiser enables them to contribute, each for individual reasons. The more important reason, however, is the personal connection. The donor must have a personal interest in the meeting with the fundraiser (otherwise, it would be easier to just get it all done on the phone or in a letter). This could be a genuine fondness, the chance to learn something new during the meeting or hear updates about issues that are of interest to the donor (before flights, I always make sure to thoroughly read the Israeli news so that I can answer complex questions about Israel from donors), or a sense of personal commitment toward the fundraiser. This is just one of the reasons a successful fundraising professional must be equipped with an array of talents in order to connect and maintain relationships with the donors.

Building and expanding a donor base. My friend Gerry Halbert from Toronto is one of the most admired fundraisers in Canada, and he donates his time and effort to his community on a volunteer basis. He has often told me, "You need to build and expand your donor base all the time." A healthy donor base is built like a pyramid. There is a wide base of smaller donors, followed by a layer of medium-sized donors in the middle, and then a few big donors at the top. Maintaining this pyramid takes time, work, and resources. For an organization that has local representations and ample staff, this is not a problem. For small or medium-sized organizations that depend on out-of-town staff that occasionally visits the target cities or countries, it is not easy to maintain this kind of donor structure. Yet in any event, even if the pyramid is small and not always built by the book, it's still important to constantly work to expand the organization's circle of donors, bringing in new people and cultivating them so that some of them will move up your pyramid.

Parlor meetings. One of the common ways of expanding your circle of friends and supporters while traveling is by holding parlor meetings. An existing friend of the organization invites friends and colleagues to hear about the cause she is supporting. The meeting can take place at an office, a restaurant, the home of the host, or a public building (YMCA, Jewish community center or local church, for example). Such a meeting gives the fundraiser an opportunity to introduce himself and his organization to several people at the same time. Attendance will usually be between five and several dozen people. Any less than that is just a meeting with a few people, and any more than that makes it feel like an official event.

When a donor hosts a parlor meeting, it's an expression of her support and commitment to your organization. Organizing the meeting involves prior work (sending out invitations, telephone calls, arranging the venue, ordering refreshments, checking that people will attend), often expenses (refreshments, hosting at a restaurant), and most of all using the donor's social credit. Someone who invites friends to a meeting with a representative of an organization that is raising money knows that the invitation will "cost her" in the future, as she now owes her friends an affirmative response to events that they may organize.

One of the main questions that always arises when a meeting is organized for exposure purposes is whether this meeting is defined as a fundraiser. The question is not just a technical one, and it has a few ramifications. When people are invited to a fundraising meeting, they usually hesitate more and are less excited about coming. They know that their participation will not only cost them their time, but their money too. In my opinion, when the purpose of the meeting is to raise money, that should be spelled out clearly; otherwise the host might be putting his guests in an unpleasant situation.

The host and the fundraiser, when organizing the event, need to decide together on the primary objectives of the meeting. They also need to decide what is more important – exposing more people to the organization's operations, with the expectation that some of them might show interest and commitment and perhaps become donors, or risk a smaller turnout, with those in attendance knowing that they are expected to donate. There is no clear answer, but it is very important to coordinate expectations, both between host and guests and between host and fundraiser.

A common but critical error that fundraisers make is not keeping in touch with people who have participated in parlor meetings or other exposure events. If the connection is not maintained, at least with some of the participants who expressed interest, the meeting was not utilized to its fullest potential. Remember to hand out and collect business cards. Write down important points that you learned from your discussions with attendees ("I'm the chairman of a philanthropic foundation, and I would be happy to talk to you more in the future…"). Send them thank-you notes and add their contact information to your mailing list. Learn additional information about important people and try to meet them during your next visit to the city. Send material about the organization to anyone who asked for it or to anyone you think could benefit from it.

Logistics and Travel Costs

Long-distance fundraising trips demand logistic preparation and significant expenses. How do you estimate the cost of a long-distance trip? Fundraising trip costs fall into four main categories: flights, accommodations, transportation, and living expenses.

Flights. The cost of international round-trip flights varies, depending on the destination and the number of connecting flights. Domestic cross-country fares also vary depending on the hour and day that you choose to fly.

Accommodations. Some people are hosted by friends or donors. The advantage is the monetary savings and the chance to develop a closer relationship with the host, but sleeping at someone else's house also has significant disadvantages. The first issue is that it deprives the fundraiser of the free time that is so important at the beginning of a busy day and at its end. It makes things even more complicated when you're suffering from jet lag because of the time difference. The second disadvantage is that there are donors who may view their hospitality as being in lieu of a donation to the organization. So while you might have saved a few hundred dollars on a hotel, you might have lost a few thousand dollars in donations.

Transportation. Until a few years ago, I pretty much relied solely on taxis to go to meetings in a certain city. But with today's navigation systems, it's easy to reach your destination in a rental car. Aside from the big cities like New York, Paris, and London, where parking is hard to find and expensive, a rental car is the best way to move around.

Living expenses. Most organizations have a set rate for living expenses with two levels: when staying at a hotel, and when not staying at a hotel. This makes things simpler for the fundraiser and for the organization, and spares them from saving receipts and documenting every cup of coffee.

Consider taking advantage of the three meals of the day for meetings with donors and potential donors. A meeting over a meal is more intimate and less rushed. Coordinate your timing based on the local customs. For example, in the United States, lunch takes about an hour, while in France, it'll take at least two hours. In North America, you can eat dinner earlier, at five or six, especially when meeting with older people, but in Europe, this is less common.

Who pays for the meal? There is no single answer to this question, but there definitely are common practices: when you meet with a donor or potential donor (who are usually financially well-off), they will almost always invite you and pick up the tab at the end. When you go out with a colleague, then as well they will usually pay for you because you are a guest in their city; you'll reciprocate when they come to visit you. In any event, offer to pay for part of the bill or at least reach for your wallet with an apparent gesture until there is an internal decision, and let them say: "This time is on me."

Be prepared for exceptions to the rule as well. I once ate a meal in one of the big cities in California with a donor who had just contributed a very large sum. He chose the restaurant where we dined, and it wasn't cheap. At the end of the meal, our joint bill was more than a hundred dollars. When the bill came, I assumed he would pull it toward him as donors usually do. But that didn't happen. When I understood that he expected me to pay, I paid without hesitating. On another occasion, when I ate with a donor who contributes hundreds of thousands of dollars a year to charity, the mutual friend who introduced us told me: "You should pay for him. He loves it. He takes it as a compliment and it makes him feel good…" I paid for dinner, and he donated $50,000.

Gifts

There are those who make the mistake of thinking that gifts for donors are a waste of time and money, but I am a staunch believer. When you come as a guest to a certain city to meet someone and ask for a contribution of time and money, giving a small, thoughtful gift adds sincerity and expresses your good intentions. It's certainly fine to invest $30 in a gift for a donor whom you plan to ask for $30,000. Choose gifts that represent the organization and its unique value and are appropriate for the timing of your visit – local olive oil, something handmade by at-risk youth, a coffee table book, or a gift local to where you live, etc.

Remember, a fundraising trip, no matter the destination, is not a vacation or a prize. Often, fundraisers complain to me that while they're spending sleepless nights in airports and on planes, sleeping in a different hotel every night, suffering from jet lag and sporadic meals, their colleagues at the office are convinced that they're having the time of their lives at the hottest tourist locations. There's no doubt that travel is magical and interesting and makes for a nice break from the daily routine. But a fundraising trip is not a family vacation – it's hard, challenging work. Sometimes, when flights are frequent, they can take a toll on your family life (you miss your spouse and children and also miss waking up in your own bed) or your health (back pain, difficulty sleeping, dryness of the skin and eyes, and other symptoms). A friend told me that after flying to the United States every week for an extended period of time, he ended up breaking out in a rash and feeling dizzy as soon as he even entered the airport.

FRIENDS ORGANIZATIONS WORKING ABROAD

One of the main challenges in managing an international fundraising system is working efficiently and in good spirit with the network of Friends organizations abroad. The Friends entity is an independent organization with legal status which enables it to receive domestic tax-deductible donations and issue tax receipts to donors. It reports lawfully to the local government and tax authorities. It is through these organizations that nonprofits from different parts of the world can raise money internationally and give tax receipts in return for the donation. The Friends organization's main goal is to promote awareness and fundraise for the homebased institution or program and then designate the money to the homebased organization.

Aside from the challenge of maintaining professional and collegial long-distance relationships with overseas or satellite offices, other innate difficulties are sometimes built in or arise in managing a team of employees and operation systems in another country. These may include differences of culture, language, time zone, currency, and law.

When I managed a fundraising division at a university, one question was constantly hovering in the air at discussions with the Friends team in the United States: Who's the boss here? Who do we report to? The day-to-day work justifiably mandated that the boss was the university president, and the director of international fundraising reported to him. But the chairman of the American Friends nonprofit asserted that his team members had to be independent. They should only have to report to Friends professionals or board members of the American nonprofit. Even when we tried to keep our eyes on the higher goal for which all of these organizations existed – promoting the university's goals, developing it, supporting students – the organizational difficulties were still bothersome at best and an obstacle at worst.

To avoid these difficulties, an effective fundraising work plan must include smooth functioning of and interface with the organization's Friends groups.

FUNDRAISING EVENTS
Everybody Loves a Dinner

I've heard the following sentence dozens of times from organization directors, with minor variations, and usually spoken with wistful looks on their faces: "I heard that X organization raised two million dollars at their dinner in New York City. Why can't we organize a dinner like that?!" It's every organization's dream: one event, hundreds of participants, lots of donations, and let's call it a day. Is that really how it works? Not quite.

Oren Heiman, a partner at Shibolet Law Offices in New York who also advises Israeli nonprofits, said that representatives of nonprofits are constantly coming to his office asking to open a branch in the United States or at least organize a dinner to raise donations. Only someone who has never organized a fundraising event could imagine that this is a simple task. "I find myself cooling their excitement and explaining to them that without a few vital conditions, it is not possible or worthwhile to hold a successful fundraising event," Oren shares. A profitable dinner is a very expensive ordeal and requires hundreds of hours of work by a range of professionals, as well as experience, skill, and years of developing and maintaining relationships with people.

By definition, the main objective of a fundraising event is to raise money for the organization, but this is not the only goal. Some additional objectives and benefits include:

- **Broadening the organization's circle of friends.** A well-organized event can attract new people who will be exposed to the organization's existence, gain familiarity with the cause, and show interest in taking part in its activities, including donating money.

- **Recognizing the organization's friends and donors.** An organization needs to know how to thank those who voluntarily offer their assistance, and a fundraising event is a great opportunity to do that. Honoring the organization's central friends and donors or prominent figures can be a great way to leverage connections by attracting new people. Examples of degrees or awards that you can bestow upon people at the event are Woman of the Year, Life Achievement, Honoree, Honorary Doctorate, Exceptional Entrepreneur, and more.
- **Creating a sense of pride and deepening donor involvement.** An evening that showcases the organization's success and contribution to society and presents the organization's achievements and future vision makes its existing friends and supporters feel proud and want to contribute even more.

There is a range of possibilities for events that can promote the objectives listed above, and hosting a dinner is just one of them. You can organize a festive event at the home of a central donor, a luncheon at a hotel, an evening around the swimming pool, a formal-dress occasion, or an event at a unique desert location. It can be a night at a bar or restaurant, or a meeting hosted at a company or office. You can serve a meal, or just drinks; the food can be fancy or homemade. It all depends on the objectives, the target audience, the style of the organization, its messages, the budget, and the people organizing the event.

Is Hosting an Event Relevant for You?

There are a few questions that need to be answered before you decide to organize a fundraising event. These include:

- What is the purpose of the event?
- Do we have the personnel to organize it?
- Do we have a budget for it?
- Is this the best way for us to raise support and money for the organization?
- Is this a good use of the management's time?

But the main question is:

- Do we have people to invite to this event?

A university with a fundraising tradition of fifty years, a hospital with a well-based Friends organization, a youth organization with tens of thousands of alumni – these organizations have a broad existing base and target audience, even if it is not always organized and contact isn't fully maintained. But a small social initiative that is just a few years old, whose donors can be counted on two hands and is not yet well known, may not have enough people to invite to such an event. If that's the case, different steps should be taken to raise support. Leave the dinner for a later stage when the organization's fundraising efforts are more fully developed.

Preparing for the Fundraising Event

There is not enough room here to list all of the logistical preparations that come with organizing a fundraising event. The type, size, and cost of the event vary based on the organization, its size, character, target audience, and budget. I would like to emphasize one point regarding the preparations: often, the fundraiser's focus turns to logistics when the doors open to the event and it begins. This is a mistake and can lead to many missed opportunities. Make sure your attention is on your guests when they start showing up.

At one of the events that I helped organize, we attracted an impressive list of new, influential people, with strong donating potential, to connect to the organization. To prepare the organization's fundraising staff, we created a chart featuring pictures and data for about twenty people, showing their background, areas of interest, family status, possible connection to the organization's activities, donation history to other organizations, and other information. Each of the senior staff members was assigned to a few of the new invitees. They would dedicate special attention to these individuals, make sure that they were exposed to the organization's activities, introduce them to existing friends of the organization also present at the event, and most of all, continue the connection with them after the event.

How did they continue to cultivate the relationships with the new potential donors following the event? They sent thank-you notes and called. They offered to host a private tour of the organization and suggested that each potential donor invite a few friends to come on the tour. They asked if and how each person would like to be involved, added them to the organization's mailing list so that they could continue to receive updates, and asked them if they knew anyone else who might want to hear about the organization. When appropriate, they didn't feel embarrassed to ask for a donation as well.

Prerequisites for Organizing an Event

Examine three primary conditions before you decide to organize a fundraising event:

1. **Does the organization have a critical mass of people to invite to the event?** Will their attendance at the event constitute a significant contribution to the organization – of money, influence, or otherwise?
2. **Does the organization have the human resources necessary to plan, organize, and carry out a respectable event?**
3. **Has the organization defined the objectives of the event and planned follow-up activities?** How will it keep up the momentum created at the event and cultivate relationships with the organization's new friends?

HOSTING DELEGATIONS AND VISITORS

A donor's visit to your organization is extremely important. The visit could be a turning point in the donor's attitude toward your organization and in your relationship.

During the first year that I established the fundraising system at Tel Hai College, I hosted a delegation of about twenty community leaders from Canada. Before they arrived, I researched and identified the major players in the delegation. Throughout the visit, I concentrated on connecting with them. This visit was the beginning of a long-term relationship between myself and the donors and friends from Canada. Ten years later, some of these individuals still recall that visit and their experiences from the first time we met.

Often, a donor will visit an organization just once. This visit is likely to be critical in shaping her impression of the site, the activities, the team, the needs, and the uniqueness of the organization. Every time you contact her in the future, that first visit will constitute her point of reference. Therefore, the fundraiser must treat donor visits with the utmost seriousness and also be capable of spreading that same level of seriousness to colleagues at the organization, who don't always understand the connection between the visit and a potential donation.

Be Prepared for Anything

I led the fundraising operations in a college named after the father of a major donor from the United States. The donor, who was on the Forbes 400 list of the wealthiest people in the United States, donated significant sums for over twenty years, but had never visited the institution. One day, he announced that he was coming to Israel with his wife for a family occasion and that he wanted to visit the institution named after his father – specifically on Saturday afternoon. On Saturdays, however, the institution is closed and completely empty.

But to such a big donor, whom we had invited to visit for so many years, it was impossible to say no. So the entire organization prepared for the donor's visit on Saturday. I observe the Jewish Sabbath, so I stayed in a hotel near the college for the entire Sabbath so that I could walk to the college, because riding in a car is not allowed by Jewish law. The decision to stay away from my family on the Sabbath so that I could attend the two-hour visit on Saturday afternoon was not an easy one. To me, this Sabbath away from home was like military reserve duty, just without the uniform and the gun. It just had to be done.

The visit that we had anticipated for so many years took place as planned. We prepared everything in advance at the institution, opened the gates, and set timers in advance for the air conditioning in the halls. Only those who had to participate were asked to be present on Saturday. The donor was deeply impressed and kept repeating that he hadn't imagined the institution this way. The connection with him was raised a level, and from that point onward, all communication with him about the institution took on an entirely different context.

Delivering a Message

It is best for the donor to directly meet the program participants or project benefactors, and not just the fundraiser. A donor who visits an organization is well aware that the fundraiser is biased and will tend to say the right things to make the organization look good. The fundraiser is usually a smooth speaker, good at presentations, and an expert in the art of marketing and sales (otherwise he or she wouldn't have become a fundraiser). But when an orphan tells her story at an orphanage or a disabled soldier tells the story of the battle in which he was injured and the help that he receives from the rehabilitation organization, the impression is completely different. The same is true when a young woman from an impoverished neighborhood introduces the start-up that she founded thanks to a youth entrepreneurship program, or when a teen from an Arab village talks about his integration into the workforce thanks to a career promotion program for minorities.

Offi Zisser, CEO of Azrieli Foundation Israel, emphasizes that a donor should see the real activities firsthand and experience them as they happen in their natural surroundings, instead of watching a staged event or edited video. In addition, Offi says, the donor should try to speak with the professionals on the ground and listen to the program's real beneficiaries, not only to the eloquent managers. She relates, "During a site visit to a renowned institution with a donor foundation I once worked with, close to twenty different executives accompanied the entire visit. One of the foundation trustees turned to me and asked, "Don't all of them have work to do?" At the same time, for the right message to be delivered at the right time and in the right manner, nothing should be left to chance. Make sure to prepare anyone who is supposed to be communicating the organization's message and explain the purpose of the visit, including background about the visitors. Don't hesitate to conduct simulations of the interaction with the donors, presenting the message and answering your prep questions, down to the smallest detail. No one has ever regretted practicing too much before an important donor visit.

Preparing for the Visit

One of the largest and most surprising donations I ever raised was from an unfamiliar international foundation. An Israeli donor told me that the foundation was looking for projects to fund, to the tune of millions of dollars.

The donor sent me a one-page document – a call for project proposals. The description of the criteria in the document fit our projects. I contacted the foundation using the email address on the document they had distributed. A few weeks later, I received a response that the foundation was interested in our projects, and the very next week, a representative of the organization contacted me to schedule a visit.

At this point, we shifted into full gear. Pulling some strings, I received detailed information about the foundation's expectations and the elements important to the representatives who would be visiting us. I used the information to prepare a document with talking points, and I gave it to the organization's president and recommended that she use it in discussions with the donors during the visit. We also simulated questions and answers to prepare in advance for challenging questions. In the end, the visit played out exactly as we had planned, like a chapter out of a guidebook for hosting donors. As answers to their questions had been practiced in advance, the right messages were transmitted, and at the end of the visit, we received a very sizable donation.

It is important to decide who will be speaking with the donors – and who won't be speaking with them, too. Remember that sometimes damage can be caused. I remember one traumatic event that happened in an organization I represented. The chairman of our board of directors, a wealthy man himself, spoke to a delegation of potential donors from overseas. He tried to enthusiastically convince them that "donating money harms the organization"! How he directed himself onto this topic was beyond anyone in the room. The management cringed in frustration and prayed that he would finish his speech as quickly as possible.

Collecting Information about the Visitors

It's a good idea to ask for biographies of the visitors. Request a copy of their itinerary and check which other organizations they will be visiting. Also collect information about the foundation or organization they are representing. If relevant, try to have a preliminary conversation with the people organizing the visit and ask what they feel is important for them to see and learn.

For example, an organization involved in youth education may discover that an important visitor is a descendant of Holocaust survivors and donates to Holocaust remembrance organizations. The fundraiser can then empha-size this point among the organization's areas of work. An organization that promotes business empowerment among young adults will certainly find it interesting that an important donor who is about to visit grew up in a poor family and credits his business success to the mentor he had at the beginning of his entrepreneurial career. The more relevant information you collect and implement when preparing for the visit, the better the chemistry and match will be between the organization's operations, vision, and needs and the visi-tor's aspirations and dreams.

What Not to Do during a Donor Visit

At all times, make sure that you are committed to the truth and avoid pre-senting a false picture to the donors. You should stay away from fraudulence at all costs. One organization held a tree-planting ceremony with its donors, only to uproot the saplings and use them at a different tree-planting site after the donors left. It took them years of effort to remedy their tainted reputation.

In addition, take care to ensure that the organization looks well main-tained and is welcoming to all visitors. I once went to visit the offices of a nonprofit organization for the first time, and I felt as if they were giving me a lesson in how *not* to host visitors. While I hadn't arrived as an official donor, it was a donor friend who asked my opinion about the organization, and the organization's directors also knew of my close connections with some of their donors.

When entering their offices, my first impression was a negative one. The organization was located in an office building in an unseemly industrial zone. Of course, a small organization cannot be expected to improve infrastructure in its location or the appearance of the office building. But it's hard to justify the fact that the sign for its small office was evidently neglected, the paint on the office's walls was peeling, the furniture shabby, and the lighting in the conference room inappropriate.

But that was just my external impression. When I arrived at her office, it turned out that the organization's CEO had forgotten about our meeting, even though I had confirmed it with her secretary. Upon my entering, she didn't even stand up to greet me or apologize for forgetting our meeting. The conference room was set with a lovely spread of refreshments, which was to their benefit, but when I asked about the refreshments, she explained that an American delegation was supposed to have visited them but cancelled at the last minute. Obviously disappointed about the money that the organization had put out, she nevertheless didn't even bother to offer me any of the abundance of neglected food.

The conference room was unpleasant as well. The air conditioner made the room so cold, I had ask her to turn it off. The meeting with the manager and her partner began, but she was engrossed in sending text messages from her phone. When I asked several questions about the organization and reached the question about the organization's financing and donation sources, she suddenly looked up startled. Staring at me suspiciously, she asked, "Why do you ask?"

No sooner had it started than I wanted the visit to end. Throughout, I tried to remind myself that the organization does important work. I imagined that maybe at that moment the director had a health problem or family issues. I tried to be patient and positive. I looked for reasons that donors would want to give money to this woman or would see her as a competent enabler for an organization. I knew that the organization had donors, and I tried to imagine myself in their shoes, as if I were being hosted at a donor visit. I came to the conclusion that perhaps the director was only nice when she thought she would get something useful out of the visit.

When I finally managed to leave, after forcing myself to remain polite and pleasant and not to tell her what I thought, I told myself that it was all for the best. This was a great negative example that I could use in my book – to show organizations how *not* to host visitors and how management should never view a visitor as a purse waiting to be opened.

Don'ts When Hosting Donors

1. Avoid misrepresentations. Stick to the truth.
2. Don't leave certain topics uncoordinated, hoping that everything will just work out.
3. Avoid giving people whose discretion you don't trust an opportunity to speak.
4. Don't make promises that you know you won't be able to keep.

5. Don't push a donor too hard. Respect the donor's privacy and the pace at which he or she is comfortable proceeding.
6. Don't be overly optimistic about receiving a donation from a visitor. A potential donor who says, "Great and special work that you're doing here! I'm sure that many people will want to help you…" isn't necessarily being self-referential.
7. Don't forget to continue to develop the relationship and do follow-up.

When hosting donors, search for the *kime* – the process of focusing and accomplishing. Work on the message that you want to transmit at the right time, place, and level of intensity. Be sure to prepare yourself carefully. Your *kime* might include that young child with the right story, the right look in his eyes, and the verbal skills to transmit it. It could be the connection with the key person in the delegation, when you introduce him to that immigrant girl whose family he met during his visit to Ethiopia. It could even be a flight in a helicopter over the college campus to get a feel for the number of students in attendance. *Kime* doesn't come from a game plan in a book or in a guide for hosting visitors. It requires preliminary information, thorough preparation, intuition, sensitivity, and originality.

CHAPTER 5

DONORS – DIFFERENT WORLDS, GOALS, AND INTERESTS

Every case is different, and every person is unique.

We've already mentioned that there are many wealthy people in the world and many foundations that have money to give out. But fundraisers have to think concertedly about whom to contact and how.

FUNDRAISING FROM PRIVATE DONORS
Who Is a Likely Donor?

What type of person might donate to my organization, and why should he or she pick me? This is one of the main questions for any organization interested in fundraising. What's called the twenty-million-dollar question: "Who will be my donor? Why should someone choose my organization out of the hundreds of others who are also requesting donations? Where will I find this donor of mine? In my own neighborhood? Across the ocean?" Look for the following traits to help you find the person (or company or foundation) who will consider donating to your specific organization:

- Personal connection with someone at the organization
- Mutual friend who will make the introduction
- Desire to influence the organization's activities and agenda
- Motivation to enhance prestige (becoming a board member, a VP, or a president of an NGO looks good on a CV and bio, and furthermore is expected of community and business leaders)

- Caring for the issue that the organization promotes
- Geographic connection (wanting to contribute to a local cause)
- Historical connection (for example, someone who once studied at a boarding school may consider donating because of fond memories and the impact the school had on his or her life; or people may wish to give to an organization their parents or grandparents gave to)

How Do I Find the Donor and What Do I Say?

I got to Donald through Ben, a friend of an American friend. The connection with Ben developed without any relationship to fundraising. My friend Alan introduced us when I started writing my first book, *Son of My Land*. Ben is an accomplished author, and his advice helped me with the process of writing my book. During one of our phone conversations, long before we met face-to-face, he told me about Donald and praised him profusely, saying that he was the most extraordinary person he'd ever met: kind, humble, bright, and visionary – an American businessman who had founded a business from the ground up and developed it for years until it grew to sales of billions of dollars. My fundraising feelers were immediately stimulated. "Could you introduce me to him?" I asked Ben. To my surprise, Ben agreed.

Six months passed from the moment we met virtually until our first meeting. I made a special trip to his city, which was in the central region of the United States. It was my first time visiting that state. In preparation for the visit and the meeting with Donald, I read his autobiography with great interest and learned everything I could about him from the internet and other sources. When we met face-to-face at his office, I felt like I already knew him. Donald turned out to be a very inspiring person: a man with a vision, admired by his employees, modest and generous. At our first meeting, I invited him to be a "pioneer investor" for an innovative project that I was developing at the time, and I asked him to give a significant donation to kick off the project. He looked me in the eye, stretched out his hand and said, "It's a deal." This meeting was the beginning of a relationship, and I returned countless times to that city, expanding the circle of donors with Donald's assistance, building a foundation of friends and donors who in time became one of the organization's central bastions of support. All thanks to a successful introduction made by a friend of a friend.

When Can I Talk about a Donation?

This is one of the questions every fundraiser contemplates. At what stage of the relationship with a donor is it possible and desirable to ask for a donation? Is it polite and proper to ask straight-out at the first meeting? Should you wait until the mutual acquaintance is deeper? Should you wait until the potential donor invites a donation request? When is the right time?

The short answer is that there is no exact time that you can point to and memorize. Every case is different, and every person is unique. The truth is that it's so much easier to sit with donors – who are usually interesting, smart people and good conversationalists – and talk to them about anything in the world other than donating to your organization! I have seen it time and time again, with my own eyes. Professors, businessmen, educators – it's so hard for them to switch from a friendly chat to a donation request. Sometimes, they feel uncomfortable, or that it's beneath their dignity. Sometimes, they want to ask but just can't do it.

Proposing marriage is referred to as "popping the question." Asking for a donation can feel similar. Even after hundreds of donation requests, I still feel butterflies in my stomach when I have to pop the question. There are donors who make it easier for hesitant fundraisers, so it's important to pick up on the signals. A question such as "So how can I help you?" might mean, "How much money do you need for the project/to build the building?" "What would you like from me?" could be an explicit invitation to ask for a donation. But there are also cases when it's worth your while to be patient.

My friend David Cohen is a British-Israeli businessman and philanthropist. One of his public positions was president of the United Jewish Israel Appeal (UJIA) in the UK. He believes that a donation request should not be rushed and that donors should be cultivated. "You need to be prepared to develop the relationship and gradually move upward regarding the amount of the donation. I never push or pressure a donor. When I was president of the UJIA, I asked a donor to contribute £ 5,000, and after a few years of building a relationship, as he became more and more familiar with the organization, he donated £ 100,000."

I met with Chris time and time again over a three-year period before I ever asked for a donation explicitly. Each time we met, it seemed to me that he couldn't figure out why I wasn't asking him for a donation. Why indeed? Because I felt that the correct approach was to build a relationship, understand his areas of interest, hear about the things that were truly important to him, and wait for the time when he felt a desire to donate on his own. It's important to also be attentive to hints and signs that really mean, "Don't ask for a donation now!" If a donor tells you during your meeting, "My business's profits have plunged," or "Unfortunately I've had to reduce my contribution amounts," he is essentially asking you not to press him for a pledge. Asking for a donation in a situation like this will put both of you in an uncomfortable position, aside from the fact that it won't lead to any results. When choosing your timing, take into consideration the atmosphere, time constraints, health situation, and other relevant issues.

An unusual time to ask for a donation was the eve of the 2013 fiscal crisis in the United States. I usually plan my fundraising trips overseas a few months in advance, so that I can schedule meetings with busy people. When I planned my trip to Cleveland, I didn't expect that the meetings I would be holding there with donors would take place amidst threats of a federal strike and an economic crisis due to the perception that the American government faced insolvency.

The federal government shutdown began two weeks before my trip, following a disagreement between the Democrats and the Republicans on President Barack Obama's health reform. Eventually, the budget was not approved, and all of the federal services shut down. The big threat was on October 17 – the date that the American government reached its debt ceiling. Not increasing the debt ceiling meant the government wouldn't be able to take loans that would continue to feed the American surplus consumption. This would mean insolvency – bankruptcy for the United States, the greatest superpower in the world. Such a horrifying storyline and its destructive impact on world economics seemed like a page out of a fantasy novel until a few years ago, but when I was in Cleveland, that nightmare seemed to be getting closer and closer. To increase the drama, the major television channels showed a stopwatch that counted the hours and minutes left until the fateful date of October 17, 2013, at midnight.

Now go ask for a donation when great America is about to go bankrupt. The financial markets could crash, funds could lose dozens of percent in value, and the ramifications are endless. But despite the bad timing, I didn't postpone my trip. I held all the meetings that had been scheduled in advance, and when it was relevant, I even asked for donations.

Over the years, I've learned that it is very hard to choose the right time for a fundraising meeting. Sometimes, it'll be too early, before the decisions are being made about donations for the upcoming year. Other times, it'll be too late, because they've already divided up the whole pie. Often, the timing is off because of health-related circumstances or a sensitive family situation, and sometimes, the donor is too busy with work matters. Timing is important, but hard to predict. Therefore, I believe that after you've managed to schedule a meeting with a donor, you should hold the meeting almost at all costs. During the meeting, try to gauge the overall situation, the donor's mood, and the financial environment. Then decide whether it's a good time to ask for a donation, or even ask to increase the contribution – or not.

What to Offer the Donor?

You've identified potential donors, contacted them, scheduled a meeting, collected information, prepared your materials, decided that the time is right to ask for a donation – now, what do you offer the donor? The answer, which is obviously not the same in every situation, usually depends on a number of factors:

- **Priorities.** Based on your organization's various needs and the donation options you've prepared, which need/project/plan/building is most important/urgent/vital for the organization?
- **Areas of interest.** What's important to the donor? What, to the best of your knowledge, will push the right buttons? What will make the donor feel sympathetic and connected?
- **History.** What have you talked to the donor about in the past? What did you propose supporting? Continuity and consistency are important as well.
- **Current events.** Are there issues on the public agenda or relevant in the local community that will make the donor feel more open to and concerned about your proposal?

Taking into account the above factors can be very helpful in your attempt to offer the right thing, at the right time, in the right place, and of course – for the right person. The attempt is not always successful, however. I have experienced quite a few donation requests where none of this worked. I suggested that the donor support a certain program, and it turned out that he actually preferred to donate toward construction (or vice versa). I thought that he didn't want to hear again about a project that we'd discussed in the past, for which he had refused to donate, but it turned out that he was in fact very interested in it and was just waiting for the right time to start donating. And so on.

This is one of the reasons that a meeting to ask for a donation requires the utmost concentration from the fundraising professional, who must utilize all of her senses and intuition. She needs to "feel" the person sitting opposite her, be super-attentive, and pick up on all the hints and signs. Sometimes, when I walk out of a meeting with a donor, I feel like I've just finished a vigorous two-hour lecture or practiced karate for three hours straight.

The Fundraiser's Commitment to the Donor

The word *commitment* or *pledge* is usually used to describe the donor's expressed intention to give a donation. But the fundraiser needs to make commitments just as donors do. L. is a longtime friend who lives in Canada. I met him when I was responsible for fundraising for a certain organization. He agreed to contribute to the organization and even convinced some of his friends to donate, and we've stayed in touch ever since. When I suggested that he contribute to a new organization for which I was working, his answer was a big compliment to me, but it also obligated me. "I will donate, and I'll keep donating to your organization – as long as you're still there." Perhaps he thought he was giving himself a way out by conditioning his donation, but I saw it as an expression of trust and mutual commitment.

A fundraiser's commitment (or that of a CEO, or anyone who is raising a donation) often crosses the boundaries of his or her tenure at a certain organization. When a donor whom I had recruited to contribute to a certain organization told me that he felt frustrated by the way the organization was treating him, I felt embarrassed and personally responsible despite the fact that I was no longer working there.

WHY DO PEOPLE DONATE?

I have often been asked, "Why do people donate? What motivates them? Why to your specific organization and not a different cause?" Most of the time, I respond with my own question, "Do you sometimes donate to charity? To cancer foundations, homeless people, or any other cause?" Usually, the answer is affirmative. Then I ask my next question, "Why? Do you enjoy donating?" At this point, the answer is usually clear. Still – why do people donate? For a range of reasons, including the following.

1. The Three Rs of Fundraising

Every fundraiser knows that donors donate to people. In this spirit, the three Rs of fundraising are Relationships, Relationships, Relationships. At the end of the day, people donate because of the person asking, and only afterward consider the cause. In a sense, this is similar to the venture capital industry. If you ask venture capital investors about the most important criterion they check when considering whether to invest in a start-up, the answer will usually be, "Because of the people leading the company. Are they capable of doing what they propose? Do they have fire in their eyes, that determination, the ability to hold on during the bumpy ride? Have they ever founded a company before? Are they working together like a winning team?"

I've heard the following statement from donors so many times: "I contribute because you asked me to," or "I'll contribute as long as you're at this organization..." My friend Leo from Canada once said to me, when I asked for a donation: "I don't know what exactly your organization does, and even where on the map it's located... I donate because I trust you." This sentence obligates the fundraiser to meet the donor's expectations more deeply than any contract or written document ever could.

2. Caring about a Certain Issue

People like to donate to causes that are close to their hearts, issues that are personally important to them. For example, I have a friend whose son is dealing with learning disabilities, so it was easy to convince him to donate to a center for learning-disabled college students; a donor who didn't go to college as a young adult was happy to sponsor others earning the college degree he never got. A leading businessman who lost his son in a car accident put his time, energy, and resources into road safety activism…and the list goes on.

3. Donating Is Enjoyable and Satisfying

My friend Bob Friedland, a businessman and philanthropist from White Plains, New York, expressed his love of donating in simple terms:

> To donate to a goal you believe in and see it become reality is simply a wonderful feeling. I donate to Unistream, an organization dedicated to teaching young adults entrepreneurial skills. When I told the teens in the program how I established my businesses, I envisioned some of them founding their own businesses one day, and I felt proud and deeply satisfied. When the organization makes its donors feel like that – so personally empowered and happy to be giving, the donations are a given, contributed with a smile.

The donor's satisfaction is shared by the fundraiser as well.

When I asked Steve Hoffman, President of the Cleveland Jewish Federation and former President of the Jewish Federations of North America, about the satisfaction of fundraising, Steve replied, "It's just a wonderful feeling to make people feel good about themselves because of their donations."

Fred is one of the leaders of the Toronto Jewish community. Among his other volunteer positions, he led fundraising efforts in Canada for Israel in 2007 (after the Second Lebanon War) that raised over $60 million. Fred shared with me the rule he follows in his personal contributions: "I see the donation as a privilege and an obligation, a moral and communal commitment. I've been lucky to have enjoyed success in my business. So I feel obligated to give back to the community. I have my own private rule about my annual contributions. I commit to giving a sum of money every year that is at least equal to the value of the car I drive." (By the way, Fred drives a new Ferrari.)

4. Guilt

I don't think that guilty feelings rank among the main reasons that people donate, but sometimes they do weigh in. For example, a businessman whose business involves other people's losses (for example, a debt collector) may want to clear his conscience with acts of charity and constructive deeds. Someone who would have liked to be more involved in community affairs but has a hard time finding the time due to her busy schedule might "make do" with a donation to causes that are important to her. Someone who didn't set aside enough time for his or her children because of a demanding career might donate to causes that promote child development.

5. Social Status

In many organizations and cultural and educational institutions around the world, monetary donations to the institution play an important role in determining the donor's social status in the community as well as the roles he or she fulfills in the organization. For example, in order to serve in a senior volunteer position in a major museum anywhere in the world, one must be a substantial donor. The chosen head of the board is almost always one of the top donors to the organization. Yet there are also exceptions to this rule. For example, a federal judge, renowned professor, CEO of a well-known publication, or fashion icon who is an excellent networker may also be appointed. But generally speaking, there is a direct, close connection between donations and the person's status in the hierarchy of the organization.

6. Tax Considerations

Tax incentives from government encourage people and businesses to donate to charity. Tax considerations constitute a factor when deciding how much to give and when, but are less related to the decision to whom to donate the money. It's pretty difficult to time donation requests based on tax considerations, but it is a good idea to remind the donor of existing commitments before the end of the calendar year, because usually, during this season (usually at the instruction of their accountants), end-of-year summaries are prepared and balances checked.

7. Influence

Gaining influence and legitimacy in the community is sometimes a factor in a donor's decision to contribute, but in my opinion, this motive is not a prominent one. This usually comes into play in donations from immigrants, the newly rich, and even from those who are having issues with the law.

Eli Lavan, a businessman from Ramat Yishai, Israel, is of Libyan descent. Lavan's two sons studied economics at a college in the north. During my first year as VP of external relations at that college, I realized that it was crucial to fundraise from local Israeli donors, with a preference for those living in the area. Aside from the money itself and what the money enabled the college to do, local support also provided an answer to those donors in Tel Aviv or overseas who ask more and more frequently, "What about the rich locals? How much do they give you?"

Eli stepped up without hesitation to help a student in need, "adopting" her with a tuition scholarship. During our long conversations, he shared experiences from his youth, growing up in a family that struggled with financial challenges. While still in high school, Eli started working to help his family, and he did not have the opportunity to go to college. Thanks to his hard work, sharp mind, and business acumen, Eli built a thriving business with his own two hands, but he never forgot the importance of higher education or lost sight of those who cannot access it due to financial problems.

I heard from Eli about the satisfaction he feels in giving to others, and I saw how moved he was by the touching thank-you letters that the student he supported wrote to him. I watched the tears well up in his eyes as he wrote another check and asked to come to the graduation ceremony when his "adopted" student received her degree. Eli is a living example of the joy of giving.

THE IDEAL DONOR – A SKETCH
Has Giving Capacity
It's simple math: in order for the organization to be able to receive a significant donation, the donor must be able to give a significant donation. Thousands of people who contribute to a wide range of charity causes live among us, but people who are capable of donating hundreds of thousands or even millions are not as common. A donor needs to be able to give.

There are donors who can give large sums on a regular basis to the organizations that are important to them, but the ability to donate so much is sometimes a one-time affair. I once met with a divorced couple from the United States. As a result of their divorce agreement and as part of their tax calculations, they had to contribute a significant sum to charity. The wife was from a kibbutz in the area where my organization was located, and her father was involved in our activities. Thus, we received a large, one-time donation from them, after which they were unable to significantly contribute again.

Giving capacity can change over time for various reasons. This can be due to a loss of assets, a drop in the business's income, or a decrease in interest rates that harms income from investments or funds. It can be the result of the sale of a prosperous business, family-related issues, or other personal issues. When asking for a donation, it is very important to assess the donor's giving capacity. Aaron's story expresses this point well.

During the first months that I worked at one of the institutions of higher education in northern Israel, an email appeared in the inbox of the president's office manager from an unknown person who asked for "a few donation options." The mysterious email was signed by Aaron Raznick. When I searched for information online about Aaron Raznick, I found very little. All that came up was that he was from California and that he had contributed a large sum to one of the universities there. This was sparse yet important information, which showed that he was a donor with significant giving capacity.

I answered Mr. Raznick by email, but instead of giving him donation options, I chose to connect with him. I tried to learn about his background and his familiarity with Israel and most importantly, what was really important to him. After a few emails, we moved to telephone calls. He told me that about fifteen years earlier, he had donated a significant sum to the Jewish National Fund that was used to build a children's playground in one of the remote communities in the Galilee. Two days later, I went to that community in the Galilee with my son Guy. I asked the local residents where the park was located and was happy to discover that Mr. Raznick's park is a central part of this vibrant community, used by the young families as a meeting point and place to play.

Guy ran to play on the jungle gym, and I took a picture of him next to the JNF sign featuring the donors' names. The next day, I sent the photos to Mr. Raznick with a description of the park, and I wrote to him what the residents had told me and how important the park was to the young community on a Galilean hill. At this point, I had already prepared three donation options based on the values important to him. He answered quickly, committing to donate about a million shekels, which he transferred to the institution over the course of a year.

About two months later, I went to California to meet Mr. Raznick for the first time face-to-face. I asked him, "How did you reach the decision to donate to us without visiting the institution even once? Did you send someone to check us out?" Aaron's response remains etched in my mind to this day: "I simply trusted you."

One of the big challenges that fundraisers face is assessing the donation potential of a private donor, company, or philanthropic foundation. Experience and gut feelings help, but the question marks are always there. At one of the academic institutions for which I fundraised, I forged a relationship with a former American professor living in Israel. He committed to help raise money for one of our flagship programs and even gave a donation himself. It seemed like an ideal situation – donating and fundraising, and with a background in academia to boot.

But after a few months of my investing a lot of time in meetings, conversations, and plans with this potential donor, it turned out that things were not as ideal as I thought. The donor was an academic professional but was not independently wealthy. He had received a significant inheritance from his late father and became an instant philanthropist. It turned out that the professor enjoyed his new status, but we, on the other hand, had to deal with three problems. One, he wasn't too happy about parting with his money and donating from his own pocket. Two, the friends he promised to bring in weren't too happy about joining him – one of them even told us that the professor was known among his friends as a miser. Three, while he was hesitant and slow about giving a donation, he quickly started pressuring me and the president of the organization to grant him an honorary degree.

I gradually realized that the damage he could cause to the organization would exceed the benefit. I called my friend Steve Hoffman, President of the Jewish Federations of North America, who is an esteemed professional and experienced fundraiser. I told him the whole story. "You don't want that kind of donor for your organization," Steve said to me. "You'd be better off ending the relationship elegantly and quickly, before it gets messy." That is exactly what we did. We did not oblige his request to receive an honorary degree, explaining that such an honor was contingent upon a very large donation, longtime commitment to the organization, and a lengthy approval process. At the same time, we continued to pressure him to serve as a personal example for his friends whom he had promised to recruit and to give a significant donation himself. Over time, this potential donor stopped contacting us.

Motivated to Donate

For a small donation, sometimes the fact that the donor was asked to give is enough of a reason. But to decide to donate a significant sum of money, a donor needs to have a good reason. The reasons are diverse. But sometimes, there are unique, captivating, and even touching reasons that donors suddenly decide to contribute to a specific cause. This was the case with Elisabeth from Sweden. One day, my colleagues at Tel Hai College, where I was responsible for fundraising, told me that an older woman from Sweden was visiting the college. She had arrived without coordinating the visit and said that she wanted to help the college.

My fundraising radar picked up the potential, and I met with Elisabeth at her Israeli vacation apartment. She told me that she was a Holocaust survivor. After the Holocaust, she left Europe and came to Israel as part of the youth immigration movement. She and other survivors were sent to Kibbutz Kfar Giladi and settled in structures that belonged to the abandoned Kibbutz Tel Hai, where the college stands today. "Tel Hai is where I was able to become human again," she told me with tears in her eyes. "Ever since, I have a warm spot in my heart and soul for Tel Hai. I want to help you raise support among the Jewish community in Sweden where I live." That was the beginning of the relationship between Elisabeth and Tel Hai College, a connection whose roots had been forged in the 1940s. The relationship turned out to be very productive for the college. Ever since, the college has hosted dozens of visits from her community and other related communities, enjoying a constant flow of donations from Sweden.

One donor from Canada donated to the center that supports college students with learning disabilities, because his own son suffers from severe learning disabilities but was able to complete university because he received the proper diagnosis and treatment. Another donor contributed to a program to advance Ethiopian immigrants after his daughter spent a few months in

Ethiopia and was exposed to the special challenges that the immigrants face. After she shared her experience with her parents, they decided to do something about it.

One of the main challenges of fundraising work is identifying the issue or area of activity that touches the heart of the potential donor. Donors will work to advance a cause that moves them. When there is a match between the organization's operations and the donor's values, the chance of receiving a donation is much higher. No less importantly, the donor will feel happy to contribute and will even thank the organization and the fundraiser for giving her the opportunity to do good for that cause.

Knows How to Give

Even when a potential donor has good giving capacity and the issues are close to his heart, he still needs to be a person who knows how to give. There are many wealthy people in the world who don't believe in giving charity. Maybe they don't recognize the importance of giving or don't feel the need to share their money with others. Or perhaps they just haven't reached the stage where they feel comfortable and confident enough to give to others. Recently, donating has become something that is expected from affluent people. It's almost considered de rigueur.

Today, there are organizations that track and report the philanthropic activity of the world's wealthiest citizens. They record the amounts that these individuals donate, the organizations they support, and their donations as a percentage of their total wealth. Giving charity has become bon ton, and that's a good thing. But there are still those who choose not to participate, and they have their reasons. It's important to try to learn about potential donors' philanthropic history, including whether they even donate at all.

Has Status in the Community

The donor's status in the community is very important. It may not change the amount of any donation to your organization, but it does impact the added value that the organization receives when a particular donor gives to you. What does that mean? Often, when I come to a new community, potential donors I meet with ask me, "Who else are you meeting with?" It's important to them to know how well I know local donors and what "level" of donors I meet with in their city. When I can mention a few of the community leaders, it puts me in a good position and gives the organization legitimacy. When I mention the names of some of the big donors, I often hear, "Wow, you're meeting with the real heavyweights."

The organization's status in general, and your status as a fundraiser in particular, is measured by the people who choose to meet with you and donate to your organization. Not only does their donation provide you with monetary support, it also gives you legitimacy and recognition. In addition, it allows you to reach additional donors. Using your connection with one person to begin a relationship with someone else is a vital tool. "During my meeting with Mr. Smith, he suggested that I call you to schedule a meeting…" It's also important to be familiar with the "give to me and I'll give to you" game that is often played in the fundraising world. One of the most important rules of the game is that when one donor invites another donor to contribute to a pet project, he knows that sooner or later, he will also be asked to donate to his friend's project. There are donors who avoid asking their friends to donate for exactly this reason. When an organization enjoys the support of a top donor in a certain community, this attracts the attention of the community institutions, especially the Jewish Federation.

An Undiscovered Gem

Many fundraisers tend to scan the lists of the five hundred richest people or the hundred biggest donors in the United States. They also obtain (or sometimes even buy) lists of foundations that provide grants. Basically, they concentrate on the famous, well-known donors. If you contact such people for a donation, you will be competing with thousands of other organizations, each of which is convinced that its project is important, worthy, and should be supported. You may actually succeed in receiving a donation, especially if you reach the decision makers directly. But the competition is fierce, the odds are not high, and relationships have already been developed with others.

In contrast, a smart fundraiser will identify donors who have not yet committed to many other organizations and who aren't surrounded by organizations competing for their attention. Gaining the trust of such donors will build relationships and raise support for your organization. This kind of relationship can be cultivated over time. Gradually you will have earned a loyal, important donor for your organization, who may also be able to help you raise additional funds.

Committed to Your Organization

In establishing fundraising operations for relatively new academic institutions, I have often met donors who have told me, "I've already committed to X university or Y institution; I'm on their board of governors and a member of their Friends organization. I cannot and do not want to be active in another academic institution." I always accepted their answer with understanding, and with a hint of jealousy too. A donor who is loyal to her organization and accompanies it as a donor and friend over the years is an asset that every organization should cultivate, appreciate, and preserve. A well-known rule in the sales world says that it's easier to retain an existing client than to gain new ones, and the same holds true in the fundraising world.

Personally Connected to You

Often, after all is said and done, the personal connection between the donor and the fundraiser is what will determine the nature of the donation, its size, and its continuity. When the donor thinks about her donation, there will usually be two important factors in her mind: those who will benefit from the donation (at-risk youth, talented athletes, female entrepreneurs, college students) and the person who asked her for the donation. During the fundraising process, a close relationship usually develops between donor and fundraiser. Personal stories are shared, secrets whispered, happy times and sad times experienced together, crises weathered with unity. A connection that starts as a seemingly business-related interaction grows and can become a long-term relationship.

Fundraisers must respect this connection and appreciate it to the point of sanctity. Never break the trust that has been given to you. Be sensitive to information that you hear, secrets that are entrusted with you, and to the damage you could cause if you are not worthy of that trust. A fundraiser must also know how to differentiate between true friendships and friendly work relationships, and sometimes this is very hard. It's a good idea to adhere to the American rule of "use but don't abuse."

Willing to Get Friends to Donate

A donor's commitment to support your organization can be measured using three main questions. One, does he make personal donations in a manner and at a level that reflects his giving capacity? Two, is he willing to offer his connections and his network to connect other potential donors who could support the organization? Three (and this is the hardest one), is he willing to offer support to the organization even after he is gone, meaning to include the organization in his will? (See "Legacy Giving" below.)

Regarding the second question, the connection to other donors, this is sometimes a donor's most important contribution to the organization he chooses to assist. One of the American donors I had the privilege of meeting harnessed his generosity for the organization I represented and didn't stop at just opening up doors for me with other donors in his community. He even cleared several hours in his busy schedule to go with me and sit at the offices or homes of his friends to tell them how and why he donates to my organization, asking them to join him. In this situation, potential donors didn't see me or my organization (which they had never heard of before) in front of them. They saw their friend and his status in the community. They saw his contributions to goals and projects that they had promoted in the past, and their commitment to him. This donor's behavior was the epitome of donor commitment.

Another donor in the United States who agreed to donate the amount I had requested also added, "What I donate to you is not enough. I want you to leave here with a bigger commitment." So he picked up the phone and called his friend, one of the wealthiest people in the city, and got him to make a donation as well.

LEGACY GIVING

What is a legacy donation?

This is a donation made through a donor's will or estate. The donation will be transferred to the organization after the donor passes away, and often only after the donor's spouse also passes away. Alan Gill found a nice way to word a request for a donor to remember your organization in her will: "Say to the donor: 'Just as you were a dedicated and generous partner in our work throughout your life in this world, I would like to invite you to continue to be our partner even from the World to Come.'"

Yet it's still never easy to talk to donors about donations left in their wills. After all, who wants to confront a person with the prospect of death? It's much more pleasant to ask people to donate money for a building they'll be able to see in two years' time than to describe the impact their donation will have after they're no longer here. But if there's one thing that's clear and definite in this world, it's the fact that we are all mortal. Therefore, fundraisers and directors of nonprofits need to be prepared to discuss this delicate topic with their donors as well.

Why do people contribute to a certain organization in their wills?

Similar to the reasons for philanthropic donations in general, there are many reasons people choose to donate in their wills. Two personal examples have remained especially vivid in my memory. George and Belinda are Canadian friends of mine. My relationship with them spanned several years and was characterized by mutual appreciation and deep affection. During one of my visits, they chose to share something personal and important with me:

> We are aware that you visit us not only because of our friendship, but also in order to do your job as a fundraiser. At the moment, we are unable to contribute to your organization significantly because of our commitments to other organizations and due to the limits of our available assets. But your investment of time and resources will not be in vain. We've decided to add your organization to our will. You should know that it's the only organization in Israel that we've never visited. We added it to our will only because of you! When the day comes and both of us pass away, a significant sum will be transferred to your organization.

I was overcome with emotion when I heard their words. It's hard to top such a wonderful compliment and sincere act of trust in the fundraising world.

Malcolm is an American friend who divides his time between his beach house in Florida and his house on the East Coast. A widower, Malcolm was in his nineties when he explained to me at one of our meetings: "I really enjoy our friendship and relationship, but at the moment, I cannot add a new organization to my list of donations. I have researched the genealogy of my family, my medical history, and the statistics. According to the scientific data I collected, I have between two and three years left to live. In a few years from now, your organization will receive a notice about a donation from my will."

A year later, I came to visit Malcom again. This time, he updated me that he had about two more years left to live... So I asked for his permission to discuss his donation. "I understand that at the moment, you can't add another organization to your donation list," I said. "But would you consider committing now to giving a certain sum from your estate to my organization? Then we will be able to recognize your donation and thank you for it now by naming the new wing that we're building after you. It would be a pity to receive a donation from you when you're no longer with us and we can't thank you for it properly."

Inheritance is an extremely delicate subject. Talking to a donor about her will too soon, or not being sensitive or tactful enough, could not only result in a negative answer, but even abruptly ruin your relationship with the donor. The conversation is difficult for both parties in most cases, so it must be approached with the utmost caution and sensitivity. I believe that on this issue, if the timing and the setting are not right, it is better to just wait and not take any action at all. Moreover – and this is perhaps the most important message in this book – above all, a fundraiser must be a decent human being. A mensch. Put the person opposite you first, before your interest in his property and donating potential.

CHAPTER 6

DONOR STEWARDSHIP

As the Hebrew Bible says, "I remembered for you the kindness of your youth"
(Jeremiah 2:2).

As I have mentioned, people donate to people, and donors donate to organizations led by people who care about them and who are dear to their hearts. This type of connection and commitment is not developed in a day, and it must be appreciated and maintained. Developing donor relations can be compared to cultivating a garden. A beautiful garden will grow and flourish only by investing effort, thought, planning, professionalism, hard work, and even love.

Donor stewardship – or more precisely, developing the connection with the donor – is essentially long-term, continuous cultivation of a relationship. This requires hard work, dedication, appreciation, and care.

NURTURING THE DONOR RELATIONSHIP

Opportunities to strengthen donor relationships can spring up unexpectedly. When I visited my eldest son at his army base in the Negev, a Friends of the IDF sign with the names of the donors at the entrance to the synagogue of the base caught my attention. The sign said that the building was donated by the family of a donor from Canada with whom I've had a friendly relationship for years. I asked my son to stand next to the sign, and I took a picture; the next day, I sent the donor the photo accompanied by the story. He was very moved, and the connection between us felt a bit stronger.

Staying in Touch throughout the Year

A common mistake is to contact a donor only when you want to ask for a contribution. Your relationship with a donor must be continuous! The manager of an organization once told me, "I don't want to bother his donors. They're very busy people, after all, and they probably already know that I want donations from them." In contrast, I once met a longtime donor in Canada with whom I had developed a strong friendship over the years. Regarding the organization that I had worked for in the past, to which he was still donating generously, he remarked:

> They [the particular organization] think that they are keeping in touch with me well. But they're not. I do receive reports about the program that I contribute to, but aside from their annual report, I only hear from them when they ask for my annual donation. Even then, they only contact me through the Jewish Federation in my city and don't have any direct contact with me. That's not how you keep in touch with a donor.

The Donor as a Member of the Family

I was once on a business trip in California, and on Saturday night, I received an email with tragic news. The daughter of a longtime friend, a big donor from a state on the opposite coast of the United States, was killed in a car accident. The funeral was going to be the next day. That same night, I unhesitatingly changed my plans and my plane tickets, cancelling other commitments so that I could fly to attend the funeral and support a friend.

When donors or friends tell me their birthday, anniversary, or any other important personal date, I immediately write it down on my calendar and then call them every year to wish them well. Twice a year, before Rosh Hashanah and before Passover, I make sure to make hundreds of telephone calls all over the world to wish my Jewish (and often also non-Jewish) friends a happy holiday. Before Christmas, I call my Christian friends. At Ramadan, I talk to my Muslim friends. When my children celebrated their bar and bat mitzvahs, I invited donors with whom I have become close. Most of them obviously could not come due to the distance, but they still felt welcome, like part of my family. When there was a severe snowstorm on the East Coast of the United

States, I called a few of the donors I know who live in that area to ask how they were doing. When I visit donors overseas, I usually bring small gifts that show my appreciation.

These are some examples. There are many others too. Every person has individual preferences when it comes to cultivating donor relationships. What is important is that this be done with sensitivity, in the right proportions, with multicultural and interreligious understanding, and most of all, with good and mindful intentions.

Barry Shrage, the legendary president of Combined Jewish Philanthropies of Greater Boston, says that regarding connections with donors, fundraisers need to forget that they are fundraisers. They must be vision driven and relationship driven, not just propelled by their desire for a monetary donation.

James Snyder, CEO of the Israel Museum and the person who is most identified with the museum's tremendous development in recent years, feels the same way about fundraising. To my question as to what percentage of his time he dedicates to fundraising, James answered decisively: "Zero percent. I don't see myself as a fundraiser. I build communities. I connect people to the vision. I show people that their donation strengthens the community and turns the vision into reality."

As the Hebrew Bible says, "I remembered for you the kindness of your youth" (Jeremiah 2:2). We must appreciate what donors have already done and not just anticipate what they might do in the future. This is a prime tenet of one of the central principles in the art of marketing, known as customer retention: it's easier to retain an existing customer than to acquire a new one. An organization with an effective and healthy fundraising system works hard to acquire new donors but never forgets its past donors.

DONATION PLEDGES

An old joke relates that robbers broke into the Jewish Appeal offices in New York and stole a billion dollars in pledges. A pledge is not cash. It is not a check or even a bond. It is simply a promise to donate. Most donations in the fundraising world of nonprofit organizations start as pledges or commitments. It is rare, especially when a significant sum is involved, for a donor to whip out a checkbook and write a large check to the organization.

When a donation commitment is given, the fundraiser gets excited and hurries to tell everyone about it. The people who are least impressed with commitments are the CFOs of the organizations. They want to see money in the bank. As far as they are concerned, "You can't pay salaries with commitments." A fundraiser knows that his reputation is strong and stable at an organization when both the CEO and the CFO celebrate the receipt of a commitment with him, instead of nodding their heads skeptically.

The commitment can be given face-to-face when the donation is requested, or in writing as a response to an email or letter. A commitment can be worded as a legal contract, a personal letter, or an oral promise. Undoubtedly, it is preferable to receive the commitment in writing, especially when the donation spans several years, which raises the chances of a misunderstanding down the road, different interpretation of the commitment, or a change in personal circumstances of the donor.

Written commitments are usually expected when working with foundations or corporations. But when it comes to private donors, it is often uncomfortable to ask for a written commitment out of concern that they might interpret it as distrust ("What, my word isn't enough for you? You need a contract too?"). In such cases, it's a good idea to at least send the donor a thank-you letter that also includes the details of the commitment, the amount, and a donation schedule. The letter can include sentences such as "I would like to sincerely thank you for your commitment to donate $100,000 a year for the next three years to our project..." In this way, despite being one-sided, the letter serves as confirmation of the commitment and the related details. It is also an opportunity to clear up any misunderstandings.

When I wrote such a letter to a donor who had committed to a new donation two days earlier, he replied that he had no recollection of such a commitment, but rather a smaller amount. Although I was upset about the loss of a commitment that I thought I had raised, I was happy that we had identified the misunderstanding at such an early stage, and not a year later. The truth is that many donors prefer and are happy to sign an official commitment letter. This type of commitment helps them track their promises and serves as a reminder to send the donation by the agreed-upon date.

The proper process for following up with commitments includes all of the following components:

- Documentation and organized tracking of the commitments
- Summarizing the commitment and its details with the donor
- Reminders when necessary
- Ensuring that the commitment is carried out

An inherent point of difficulty in the fundraising process is following up with the donation – translating the commitment to money in the organization's bank account. It is easy to fall for the temptation of getting excited when you receive a commitment but failing to follow through because of a lack of self-discipline or organizational discipline. This may result in commitments not coming to fruition. It is very important for the fundraiser to continuously and carefully monitor donor commitments to the organization. Foundations are usually organized and even send reminders to the organizations receiving the donations, but private donors should be reminded that the date for sending their donation has arrived.

I prefer to ask for a donation and even to remind a donor that the date of the commitment has arrived in a face-to-face meeting or at least a phone call, and not with a letter. This allows me to sense the donor, overcome any difficulties, prevent misunderstandings, and sometimes even increase the donation amount. However, this isn't always possible, especially when an organization has a large number of donors scattered all over the world.

What Happens When a Pledge Is Not Fulfilled?

There's a reason that donation commitments are not the same as an actual donation. I once received a donation commitment from a Canadian donor during a large event. It was a joyous occasion at an upscale hotel in Toronto, and the alcohol was flowing freely. I was introduced to the donor during the party by a Canadian friend of mine with whom I went to the event. A few weeks later, I called the new donor to clarify the donation transfer details. But the donor had no recollection of making any commitment to donate. He wasn't denying it. He simply didn't remember anything from that entire evening.

On another occasion, I met with an Israeli donor at his company office, together with senior members of his staff, and he committed to donate. A few months later, I called him, wrote to him, and tried to follow up with the donation, but he avoided my calls and didn't reply to my letters. After chasing him for months, I finally found out from one of the people on his staff that he had backed down from his commitment and wasn't going to donate. That happens sometimes. Perhaps the donor is having financial problems or regretted the commitment. But I thought that it would be proper for him to at least explain and notify me in a respectful manner, instead of avoiding me and wasting my time.

Multiyear versus One-Year Donations

A commitment can be for one donation or for a multiyear donation. Multiyear donations have a few clear advantages:

1. **Larger commitment.** A donor who can and wants to donate $50,000 a year can commit to donating a quarter of a million dollars over the course of five years.
2. **Improved planning.** Long-term commitments give the organization the opportunity to organize its financial plans for several years ahead by ensuring an existing base of donations for the fundraising efforts that begin anew each year.
3. **Fewer requests.** A multiyear donation commitment minimizes the need to pursue the donor every year for a gift.

But multiyear commitments also include disadvantages for the fundraising organization. Among other considerations, multiyear donations "lock in" the donor and the organization and limit the fundraiser's ability to try to increase the amount of the donation. For example, if a donor has committed in advance to a $10,000 donation per year for three years for a certain project, it will be hard to approach him after just two years and ask him to consider increasing the amount to $15,000. The answer will probably be, "Let's talk after I finish my current commitment."

Another disadvantage is that while this enables the donor to donate relatively large amounts to projects such as buildings, the donation is less significant when it is translated into an annual sum. For example, a donor can get a building named after her that costs one million dollars by donating "just" $100,000 a year for ten years. During that decade, the building will have already been constructed before the organization receives the full amount in its bank account.

A Pledge to Solicit Other Pledges

An American donor once agreed to my request that he raise a million dollars to build a building that would bear the name of his community. The understanding between us was that some of the donation would be coming from his pocket too. Indeed, that is what happened, and he committed to donate almost half the total amount himself. For a period of about two years, I met with a series of his friends with whom he connected me as potential donors. Sometimes I tried to meet them but didn't succeed. A commitment with this type of donor does demand more of a time investment from the fundraiser, but it comes with other important advantages. Each new potential donor, even if not immediately committed to giving a donation, is another potential contributor to the organization – if not today, then maybe tomorrow. He or she also comes with new circles of friends and joins the ranks of donors that every fundraiser wants and needs to develop.

Overhead from Donations

The more sophisticated, transparent, and involved the philanthropic world becomes, the greater the tendency of donors to avoid making pledges to general operational expenses. Instead, the more common trend is designated gifts: specific projects and defined programs that are outlined, budgeted, and presented to the donor. This makes financing the general operation of the organizations more difficult, since many nonprofits function based largely on donations, or even only on donations. They find themselves lacking the vital monetary resources to finance their core operations.

To solve this issue, a certain portion of the donations to designated projects should be set aside to cover the organization's general overhead expenses. There are foundations and donors who permit allocating a certain percentage of the donation amount for overhead purposes. To the dismay of CFOs and CEOs, these donors are a quickly disappearing species. The typical donor doesn't usually like to see the words "overhead expenses" in the donation request budget or in reports received about a donation. This term has a negative connotation that sounds like "money that goes to undefined purposes and to pay inflated salaries."

WHEN THE MONEY COMES IN – FOLLOWING UP A DONATION

Have you received a donation commitment? Followed up with the commitment, and the donation was made to the organization? Now, you need to follow up. In other words, you need to do what you promised would take place after receipt of the donation. There are a few points worth remembering in this respect:

1. **Fulfill your promises.** Be faithful to what you presented and promised to the donor. If you raised a donation for a building, use it to finance the construction. If the donation was meant to provide scholarships, the money must be earmarked for students. If the donation was for purchasing equipment, buy the equipment. If changes were made to the original plan that you presented to the donor (and there are almost always changes), let the donor know about them; if they are significant, perhaps ask for the donor's permission first. In short, be serious about your trustworthiness as a fundraiser and the integrity of the organization that you represent.

2. **Give ongoing updates.** Make an effort to continue to update the donor regarding how his donation is impacting, helping, and making a change for the better. A common mistake is forgetting the donor after the money arrives. That's not the way it should be. This is the stage when the donor is already connected to the organization, pays more attention to the organization's announcements, and is more attentive to its affairs. Take advantage of this for your organization's benefit.

3. **Look out for the donor's interests.** See yourself as her representative at the organization. The CFO, project manager, or CEO have less of a connection with the donor and less of an understanding of fundraising. They may unwittingly allow things or make decisions that constitute a breach of the agreement (whether written or not) between the donor and the organization, so stay on top of what's going on.

Connection between the Donation and Recipient

One of the donors who contributed a scholarship for a specific college student told me that he developed a sense of commitment to that student's academic success over the years: "I felt that it was literally my responsibility to see her complete her studies successfully and join the workforce." An organization's ability to present and report about the contribution of a donor in the context of a specific person or program is vital to creating that sense of satisfaction and ongoing commitment in the donor's heart. This makes the donor feel connected and committed to the recipient of his donation.

Reporting during the Process

As we saw above, it is essential to cultivate the relationship with the donor. Don't wait for the required reporting dates stated in the donation agreement or for the donor's request for an update. Raise the possibility of an ongoing relationship with the donor and create opportunities for her to be involved in the activities that are taking place thanks to her donation. Such reports might include a photo from an activity, a short video clip, or newspaper clippings published about the organization. Send the donor documentation of an interesting meeting with someone who has benefited from the donation, documentation of the construction progress of a building to which he has contributed, and more. But don't exaggerate with the frequency: a donor who receives an update every week is liable to feel overloaded and become bored.

Thank You!

These two simple words constitute one of the strongest tools you have in fundraising. I believe that you can't say thank you too many times. Always remember that the donor doesn't have to give anything, yet has chosen to do so. Also remember that there are a lot of wealthy people in the world who decide not to donate. Recognize your donors and know how to thank them. Thank every donor – the one who gave a million dollars and the one who gave eighteen dollars.

When my son Ari celebrated his bar mitzvah, he knew that, like his siblings, he would be expected to give part of the money he received as gifts to charity. Due to his curiosity and interest in the Holocaust, Ari chose to donate to Yad Vashem – The World Holocaust Remembrance Center. The amount he decided to contribute was a significant percentage of the money he received, and a large sum in a thirteen-year-old's terms, but in Yad Vashem's terms, it wasn't a very big donation. When we contacted Yad Vashem to coordinate giving the donation, Ari thought that Yad Vashem wouldn't pay him too much attention, but they surprised him. Their fundraising staff received his donation with the utmost seriousness and appreciation, making sure to thank him again and again and note the great significance of his contribution. They gave him a VIP tour of the museum and a certificate of appreciation, and they put him on their mailing list so they could stay in touch.

Preparing Reports for Donors

You might think that the moment a donor has transferred the funds, the fundraiser's goal has been reached. In fact, the first donation is just the beginning of the connection. Comparing this to a romance, this is the end of the courtship and the beginning of a serious relationship. With that in mind, preparing reports for donors achieves a few primary objectives:

1. **The donor expects them.** Without a report, there's no donation. Sending reports that share how the donation was used is usually a condition stipulated by foundations, but even private donors request or at least expect that you send a report.
2. **They nurture the donor connection.** A report is a wonderful recurring opportunity to update donors about what is happening at the organization and specifically with the programs for which the donor has contributed. Hopefully, such summaries will strengthen their interest and personal concern for the organization, its activities, and its objectives.
3. **Reporting stimulates review.** The process of preparing reports is in itself useful to an organization, helping it to compare its results with its goals, as well as to ensure that the money is being used for the purpose for which it was designated. This is also helpful in planning how to continue various programs.

Reports to donors come in a variety of shapes and sizes. The most common format is of course written reports, but creativity is encouraged – reports can include video clips, slideshow presentations, a recording, a song, a work of art, a dance, and more.

When a foundation or a donor requests a certain format for the report, adhere to the donor's specifications carefully, and then add something extra.

Guidelines for Donor Reports

A. Less is more. Don't use five hundred words to say what can be said well in a hundred words. Respect the time of the person who has to read the report.

B. Modesty is the best policy. Don't give your organization baseless compliments. Claims such as "Our program is the best in Israel" or "The results of the project were excellent" do not impress the experienced reader. A positive evaluation must come from the data itself, as objectively as possible, without exaggeration. For example, "In a survey conducted by the Ministry of Education, our program ranked first place" or "The annual goal of our program was 85 percent attendance, and we are happy to report that at the end of the year, we had reached 91 percent attendance." Beyond mentioning achievements, says Offi Zisser, CEO of the Azrieli Foundation in Israel, "I appreciate grant recipients who also share weaknesses, challenges, and how they plan to tackle them."

C. Share anecdotes. There's nothing better than real, personal stories from those who benefit from the organization's programs. Instead of talking about "people," "children," or "entrepreneurs," talk about Amber, Noah, and Ross. Let them and their personal stories be testimony to your success.

D. Be professional. Maintain a high level of professionalism in writing and submitting your report. Use correct spelling, grammar, punctuation, terminology, pagination, and design. While you don't have to use glossy paper and expensive designs, whatever you submit needs to be clean, fluid, without mistakes, and prepared with care.

E. Personalize it. A personal, unique report that warms the heart of the donor is always best. Don't suffice with what is expected or required of you. When I visited my brother Amichai at Kishorit Village for adults with special needs, he told me about their vineyard and successful winery. Knowing that my friend David G. from Great Britain was one of the main donors, I called him in London and told him all the good things I'd heard about the winery, whose construction was facilitated by David himself. This wasn't a report about a donation given to my organization, but rather to another organization. I had no obligation to do this, but one can only imagine how happy the donor was to hear about it specifically from me.

DONOR RECOGNITION

Donor recognition is the way that the donation is mentioned and the donor's identity acknowledged, whether in writing or via other means. It is true that Judaism praises anonymous donations to charity, and the scholar Maimonides ranks anonymous donations as the second-best form of charity (the first is the type of charity that enables its recipient to achieve financial independence). But in the art and science of modern fundraising, donor recognition is very important.

Reasons for Donor Recognition

The reasons for acknowledging a donor are twofold – the donor's reasons for wanting it and the organization's reasons for doing it.

The donor's reasons often include the following:

1. **Pride.** This is only human nature. It definitely raises your spirits to see your name featured prominently on a building, program name, letterhead, or wing of a university.
2. **Establishing a family tradition.** Many donors with whom I have discussed the philanthropy of the next generation are concerned about their family members and children continuing their philanthropic work. Some of them actively invest time and resources in teaching their children and grandchildren the art of giving charity. Mentioning a donation and the names of those who gave it acknowledges their generosity and sets a precedent for the next generation.
3. **Setting a personal example.** I have often found myself convincing donors to let me recognize and mention their names and their donations. A good example is the case of L., a modest Israeli donor who prefers to hide from the spotlight. When he donated scholarships for underprivileged students at my college, he told me that he feels no need for his name to be mentioned. "Mentioning your name is important to us because people will know that a local donor contributed generously to our organization. This serves as a model that other Israeli donors may want to mimic when they hear about it and also helps us answer those overseas donors who are constantly asking us why wealthy Israelis aren't donating more." I asked him to allow us to mention his donation publicly, and he understood and agreed.

When does this not apply?

It is not always advisable to run to announce a donation or a donor's identity. There are disadvantages as well. Public recognition of a donor is liable to expose his donation and lead to unnecessary pressure. When I raised a large donation in the United States, the editor of one of the city's newspapers asked me to write a long article about the donation to my organization. I urged her not to publicize the matter, because I believed that the organization would not benefit from such an announcement. This was a relatively new donor, and the donation to my organization was the first donation he had ever given to an overseas organization. Unnecessary publication of the fact would have only encouraged dozens of other organizations to come running to his door and would have created unpleasant competition to win his attention and benefit from his generosity. I asked my colleagues not to mention the donor's name either, even in internal conversations and memos. As long as the donor himself was not concerned about receiving recognition, I didn't think that we should hurry to announce and recognize him publicly.

How to Effectively Recognize Donors

There are so many different ways to recognize a donor. The most common are with a sign on a building or naming of a hospital, school, university, playground, scholarship program, laboratory, or project. There are donors who actually prefer recognizing someone else with their donation, such as their parents or grandparents. For example, in southern Israel, there is a building named after a well-known fundraiser who passed away at a young age, and his friends decided to commemorate his name the same way that he commemorated the names of so many others for years.

When planning how to recognize a donor's contribution to your organization, it is a good idea to pay attention to a few factors.

1. Proportionality. It would not be proper for a donor who gave $20,000 to see his name prominently displayed on a building, while a donor who contributed a million dollars is mentioned on a small sign at the entrance. When deciding the donation opportunities and levels of recognition, it's a good idea to establish how different donation quantities will be recognized. For example, in preparing a pamphlet about contributions for the construction of a building, the giving opportunities can be listed according to the different parts of the building and their importance: the entire building – $2 million; the central wing – $1 million; the auditorium – $500,000; the foyer – $300,000; the garden at the entrance of the building – $100,000, and so on.

2. Maintenance and sustainability. When planning how to recognize a donor, consider how things will look after you are no longer at the organization, ten or twenty years from now. This applies to a sign, an annual event such as a race or a lecture in memory of someone, scholarships awarded on a yearly basis, an art or educational program, or a community event. One of my biggest fears in my relationships with donors is promising something that has a good chance of disappearing in the future. Therefore, the recognition should be arranged in a manner that is professional and will endure (if it is a sign, use durable materials). Make sure that it is firmly fixed in the organization's operations (for example, an annual scholarship award ceremony at the same time each year, budgeted from a definite budget or a permanent endowment). Document it with the necessary papers (a donation agreement), and most of all, avoid making exaggerated promises that you cannot guarantee will be kept.

I once hosted a former kibbutz member who had been living in North America for many years. When she entered the college building where my office was located, she looked at the nice flooring in the building and the modern design and commented that the building was "too fancy." I wondered to myself if she would have felt the same criticism about a building in North Tel Aviv, and I answered her with a quote: "Nothing is too good for the poor." I explained to her that it was important to us to give our students, many of whom come from underprivileged backgrounds, the chance to learn in an aesthetically pleasing and respectable environment. To my worried colleagues who were concerned about her negative reaction, I said that most of the time, donors prefer to envision the building named after them as part of a complex that looks respectable, is well maintained, and honors the donor's name with its appearance.

3. Sensitivity and coordination with donors. When recognizing donors, an organization must be wary of getting into situations where it means well but actually puts its foot in its mouth. Recognition and commemoration are sensitive issues and must be treated as such. Not every donor wants the family name on a sign or in the news. If they are interested, ask them how they would like it to be done, whose names should appear, how to correctly spell their names, and if the donor himself or the entire family should be mentioned. I clearly recall a large donation that I almost lost because the donor was offended when we asked him to shorten the name that was supposed to be written in huge letters on the wall of the building. Only while doing the damage control did we find out that the long name, which included a middle name as well, wasn't even the donor's own name – it was the name of his deceased father.

4. Guarding privacy. There are donors and foundations who avoid exposure and even condition their donation on the organization's commitment that they won't mention their name. A large foundation that gave my organization a seven-digit figure stipulated in the contract that their name must not be mentioned at all. It was so important to them that they avoid the publicity that had the organization made a mistake in this regard, we would have lost this huge donation.

5. Slip-ups when recognizing donors. When I managed a university fundraising operation in Israel, an ongoing crisis with one of the families who donates to the university and lives in the central United States was brought to my attention. The family had donated a sizable sum of money twenty-five years ago, and in exchange, a sign had been installed on one of the university buildings. Many years later, members of the family came on a trip to Israel and wanted to show the younger generation the building that was named after their family. They came to the institution without notifying anyone beforehand, and when they got there, they discovered that the building was still there, but the sign was gone.

I did some research and found out that the building had been renovated, and during construction, the sign above the building had been taken down and never restored. It seemed like this was a simple problem to solve: make a new sign and attach it to the wall. I also discovered, however, that the name of the family had been placed on one wing of the building and not on the entire building, while another wing of the building featured the name of a different family.

The aggrieved family was furious. This conflict had been ongoing for over a year before I was working at the organization. As time went on, the family's frustration and anger grew, and the antagonism kept rising. At this point, I was asked to help the university's representative in North America to solve the problem. After studying the entire affair, I traveled to the city where the family lived. At their request, the meeting was scheduled at the office of one of the family members who was handling the matter. The fact that the family insisted on meeting in an office (and not over lunch or at the family's home) signaled that they were preparing for a conflict. When I entered the office, an Israeli man was also sitting there and was introduced as someone "helping them understand the Israeli mentality and the way Israelis do business." There was definitely tension in the air.

I understood that I had to deflate the hot air from their historical balloon of anger, otherwise it would be very hard to make peace and leave with a solution to the problem. I asked to open the meeting and introduced myself by saying, "I came here after a full day of flights, for the sole purpose of doing one thing: apologizing on behalf of the leadership of the institution for the agony, disappointment, and frustration that was caused to you. Please accept my apology." If anger were visible, I would have seen a red cloud dissipating from the room. "This is the first time that someone has bothered to apologize to us," the representative of the family said. From that point on, we started talking about possible solutions and left the anger and frustration behind.

CHAPTER 7

DEVELOPING PARTNERSHIPS AND ALLIES

"A single hand cannot clap."

An Arabic proverb says, "A single hand cannot clap." A smart NGO leader who succeeds in enlisting organizations, foundations, donors, and government entities to realize organizational dreams and objectives, motivating them to reach these goals together, will achieve much more than could ever be accomplished alone.

CREATING STRATEGIC PARTNERSHIPS

Strategic partnerships with a philanthropic foundation or donor mean that the relationship between donor and recipient is not short-term and is not just expressed by a transfer of money. Partnership means defining and working together to reach shared goals and to connect with more partners. It means investing in the organization's infrastructure, not just in one project or another. It means shared responsibility for the plan and its implementation.

Who Are Your Potential Partners?

Partnerships between organizations can exist to respond to a whole range of needs, not only in the context of fundraising and donations. For now, we will focus on partnerships whose main purpose is fundraising. A potential partner who is suitable for a nonprofit organization and interested in realizing an ambitious dream will meet many of the following criteria:

- **A strong financial basis.** This allows investment in other organizations as well.
- **Cash flow.** Fluid assets do not limit investment to a one-time donation.
- **The right reasons.** Partnerships should be appropriately motivated – that is, not by narrow-minded or diverging interests that could damage the organization and its operations.
- **Interpersonal chemistry.** The main players and the management of the organization should be able to work well together as a team.
- **Legitimate reputation.** The partnership should help the organization's name and reputation (receiving a donation from someone accused of a crime, for example, may deter other potential donors).
- **Partnership relationship.** An organization that will claim all the credit for a project's success or boast its name on the walls of a new building may have difficulty developing partnerships with additional organizations.
- **Stable leadership.** Leadership should not be changing too frequently, so that long-term partnerships can be developed.
- **Lack of competitiveness.** Partners should not be direct competitors. Two banks, for example, may have difficulty partnering to finance a project, since they are market competitors.

The Importance of a Partnership

The need to develop partnerships between organizations and donors to achieve shared goals is fairly obvious. To put it briefly, such a partnership:

- **Pools together resources** – financial, human, structural, and more
- **Creates a network** that is broader and enables more comprehensive access to resources
- **Increases the level of legitimacy** of the activity, since it is shared by several partners and on the agenda of more than one organization
- **Divides the burden** of executing the activity between the different partners
- **Enables expression** for different organizations and lets them bring to the table their best abilities and resources

Strategic Collaboration with Foundations

A foundation can be much more than a financial supporter. Whether due to a clear policy or because the circumstances led to it, foundations can sometimes be active, dominant partners in building and developing the organization. A significant philanthropic foundation that is a strategic partner of the organization, especially during its early stages, can offer much more than a monetary donation. How? For example, their donation legitimizes the organization in the eyes of other donors. They can recruit other foundations and donors to join them in supporting the organization, and they can even provide services such as planning, construction, marketing, and more.

When we established a new campus at Tel Hai College, the Rashi Foundation was this type of partner. The foundation was responsible for planning and managing the construction of the campus (in conjunction with professionals from the college, of course) and was the entity through which some of our donors transferred their donations. Equally important was that the Rashi Foundation's involvement provided us the legitimacy and stamp of approval for many domestic and international donors.

The Challenges of Partnerships

Creating and maintaining partnerships is not easy. Sometimes an organization is even better off working alone, choosing to forfeit the benefits of partnerships. It's often best to start operations alone and invite partners to join only after the organization is strong and stable, with proven success and an established direction. Recruiting partners for nonprofit organizations (or any organization) requires taking into consideration other people's opinions, interests, and agendas. This could hinder progress, and interpersonal tensions within partnerships could even interfere with an organization's operations.

Shlomo Dushi, CEO of Sheatufim, an international organization established in Israel to foster dialogue and connections between nonprofit organizations, government offices, and philanthropists in Israel, Europe, and the United States, offers a broad perspective on the issue of partnerships:

> Partnerships between organizations have advantages as well as challenges. The main challenge is the need to balance and compromise between different interests, priorities, and worldviews of organizations

and key figures within them. The main advantage is collective impact: the ability to combine strengths, influence, and resources to achieve ambitious goals on a large scale. In addition, a coalition of organizations means an advantage in raising funds for an initiative or program.

In general, in the world of philanthropy I observe a tendency to prefer coalitions and partnerships, comparable to the coalitions formed among government, the business sector, and the third sector, over the individual work of a single organization. I see this as a growing trend.

VOLUNTEER LEADERSHIP

Another natural source of allies in your fundraising mission is the volunteer leadership of your organization. They are a resource that should not remain untapped. When building or refreshing the volunteer leadership of an organization, it's important to plan and define in advance what their roles will be, what is expected of them, and who is most suitable to fill these positions. One of the common mistakes nonprofits make is that the managers or founders of the organization first recruit their friends to fill the positions on the executive committee, board of governors, or board of directors (as volunteers). Later, they complain that their friends are not doing the jobs that were expected of them.

In advising organizations on the topic of developing and managing volunteer leadership, we use the five Ws model to define the desired qualities in the ideal board member:

1. **Wisdom.** Intelligence, experience, knowledge, understanding. This is a person who brings skills and knowledge relevant to the organization's area of activity. For example, an organization involved in preventing violence among teens would benefit from having among its volunteer leadership a professor from a relevant field or someone with vast experience running violence-prevention programs.

2. **Wealth.** Money, funds. One of the primary roles of an organization's board of directors is to give and raise money. There is no better way to raise money than to give it yourself. In order to donate, two conditions must be met: you need to have something to give, and you need to want to give. Wealthy people can donate and are usually connected to other

wealthy people who can be recruited for the cause. It is important to mention that having money does not always guarantee a willingness to part with it on behalf of the organization. If possible, it's a good idea to coordinate expectations and let the wealthy person understand that he or she is also expected to be a donor, and not just to assist in raising money from others or help by giving advice based on areas of expertise.

3. **Work.** The willingness to work and put in effort. Board members need to invest their time and work hard without receiving anything in return: attending meetings, making phone calls, fundraising, participating in the organization's activities, and traveling, sometimes even abroad.

4. **Wired.** Connections. One of the roles of volunteer leadership is connecting and forging relationships with donors, partner organizations, government offices, media outlets, advisors, and more, and opening doors to these people and opportunities. Among your volunteer leadership, it's a good idea to have people who are well connected and capable of opening doors for the organization and its leadership.

5. **Wow!** The wow factor, a name that arouses excitement. An organization that is capable of boasting that its board of directors includes a former president of the State of Israel, Nobel Prize laureates, an Olympic champion, a famous singer, a military chief of staff in reserves, and perhaps even the founder of Google can definitely get a few "wows" to its credit. This wow factor has a few positive effects. It creates immediate legitimacy for the organization ("If so-and-so is on the board of directors, it must be a pretty serious organization"). It encourages new people to join the ranks of these famous supporters, and it opens the ears of the listener to pay attention and consider making a donation.

It's hard to envision a volunteer who meets all five of these criteria. But if you have good people among your volunteer leadership who meet two or three of them, you're doing great.

One more thing. Over the years, I learned that when I present this model to potential board members, an amusing bit of irony emerges: while most people say that they would like to count themselves among those who possess wisdom, deep down they would prefer to be among those with wealth, and if possible, they'd like to be considered "wow" personalities too.

Building a Board of Directors

How do you build an organization's volunteer leadership? I have witnessed dozens of attempts to form or upgrade a board of governors or directors that started with these types of statements: "Okay, guys. Let's see, who knows good candidates that we can recruit?" "Who do you think will agree to join our board of directors?" "So-and-so has a lot of money. We should ask him to join us." "So-and-so retired from the army last year at the rank of brigadier general and is looking for something to do. Let's invite him." "My wife's friend writes for the newspaper and can give us a lot of press; let's invite her." "So-and-so is a friend of our CEO's cousin, and knows someone at the ministry of finance who could help us meet our budgets."

Like many other things in life in general, and in our professional lives in particular, this process can be managed in a planned, organized manner. I recommend using the following steps and answering these questions:

1. Clarify the legal aspects of formulating the statutory body: How many people need to be on the board? Who are the position holders that the organization needs to have present and on which occasions? At what frequency does the board need to convene? What is the body's authority?

2. What are the body's primary tasks? For example, the executive committee of a nonprofit organization needs to meet more frequently and perform more practical tasks, like approving the budget, in contrast to a board of directors, which meets less frequently and has a less hands-on role.

3. Create a table with the criteria for recruiting volunteer leadership. The following table is an example of the criteria of a board of governors for a nonprofit and describes the relevant candidates:

Name	Ability and willingness to person- ally give philan- thropically	Ability to raise funds	Special expertise or willing- ness to help in areas important to the orga- nization's development	Special status in fields important to the organiza- tion (Nobel Prize laureate, former prime minister, for- mer minister of education, mayor)	Name and status that will attri- bute legiti- macy to the organization
Joseph Russo	X	X			
Owen Smith			X		
Jessica Harrison				X	X
Rachel Chu		X		X	X

4. Decide what the optimal number of members is and the correct balance of people representing the various areas mentioned above – with representation of women, minorities, local residents of the organization's home base, etc.
5. Compile a list of expectations of members of the board of governors: what authorities do they possess, what are their responsibilities, what level of attendance is expected at periodic meetings, what is expected of them in terms of fundraising, etc.
6. Divide up the task of having introductory conversations with potential board members and recruiting the board members among the organization's leadership and several existing friends, such as partner organizations, the chairman of the board of directors, and a major donor.
7. Set up meetings with suitable candidates, clarify expectations, and recruit them as volunteer leaders of the organization who are aware of the purpose and reasons for their recruitment and know what is expected of them.

Cultivating Volunteer Leadership

One of the most common complaints of board members, governors, and other members of volunteer leadership forums is "I feel like a rubber stamp," or "They're not giving me anything to do." It's not enough to recruit volunteer leadership; you also need to cultivate them and assign them tasks. In short, cultivating your volunteer leadership involves:

1. **Notify and update.** Keep them in the picture. Send them updates of activity. Share information, news, media coverage about the organization, and personal stories with them. Call them occasionally. Meet them for lunch from time to time – at least the leading members.
2. **Consult with them.** Ask them what they think. Utilize their experience and expertise. Share thoughts and plans with them.
3. **Involve them in decision-making processes**. Don't merely ask them to sign on decisions that the management has already made. Sometimes this makes the process longer, but it's usually worthwhile.
4. **Give them appropriate tasks.** Utilize your volunteer leadership's skills, connections, and desire to contribute – whether this involves work teams, opening new doors for the organization, fundraising, or helping with projects.
5. **Develop a personal connection.** Like cultivating donors, here as well, there is nothing that can replace personal connection. A telephone call to wish them a happy holiday, attending happy occasions or sad ones, and inviting them to activities and events are all part of that, as well as an overall attitude of caring and attentiveness.

Some organization managers prefer a weak volunteer leadership, the kind that resembles a rubber stamp approving the management's decisions, who won't "intervene and bother us," as they put it. In principle, a strong executive committee, board of governors, or board of directors can and should contribute to the organization's healthy development, not to mention the legal aspects and roles of volunteer leadership. But the reality is that it is convenient for a CEO or president, especially one with shaky self-confidence whose decisions aren't clear-cut in gray areas, when the governing body isn't "too" strong or active.

At one of the organizations that I advised, the board of directors and its composition were clearly weak. The board's primary role was not to bother the CEO of the organization. Anyone who was too strong, opinionated, energetic, or talented was deemed likely to get too involved in the manager's activities and decisions; therefore, such people were either not invited in the first place or pushed out of the ranks of the organization's volunteer leadership. Of course, the involvement of these volunteer leaders in assisting the organization's fundraising efforts was negligible. They did not have the strength, ability, or motivation to help.

Monetary Contributions from Volunteer Leadership

My Canadian friend A., a businessman and philanthropist, told me the following story about the contribution of volunteer leaders:

> When I was chairman of the board of a large Jewish organization in my city in western Canada, I would sometimes try to convince members of the board of directors to make a donation to the organization themselves. Edward was considered a tough cookie. Despite his financial capabilities and successful business, he refused to donate to the organization. I met him for lunch and asked him to give a respectable donation as one of the volunteer leaders of the organization. I explained to him that it was one of our roles as the volunteer leadership.
>
> He replied that as far as he understood, making a monetary donation was not our task. Our job as volunteer leaders was to donate our time to the organization and convince other people to donate. I chose not to argue with him about the principle, and instead said, "If so, I'd like to ask you to resign from the organization's board of directors, so that you can make a personal donation, as a donor and not as a volunteer leader."

David Cohen of the UK emphasized the importance of the personal donation of members of the volunteer leadership. "Once I met with a board member of a nonprofit. He asked me to donate to his organization. I asked him how much he himself donates to the organization in which he volunteers, but he hesitated and wouldn't answer me. 'If you won't tell me how much you donate to an organization that's so important to you,' I said to him, 'how can you expect me to donate to it?'"

The personal donation of members of the volunteer leadership of each nonprofit organization is important for three reasons. First is monetary support of the organization's activity by those who have chosen and were chosen to lead the organization. If they don't think it's important, why should others do so? The second reason is giving a personal example. A significant donation by volunteer leaders, according to personal ability, paves the way for other donors. The third reason is that someone who gives himself will do a better job when he asks others for their donation. I often find myself telling volunteers who want to learn how to ask others to give: "First give yourself, and then it will be easier to ask from others."

Per-Ake Eliasson, leader of the Kristet Center Church in Örebro, Sweden, has a unique approach to the monetary donations of his community members. When he drove me to the Stockholm airport after a conference on "The Other Israel," Per-Ake told me that he chooses not to know the size of the donations each of his community members makes. "I don't want to mix up the size of a member's donation with the attention I give him. I ask my collection staff not to tell me how much each person gives. From my point of view, all members of the community are equal, without relation to their financial contribution."

FUNDRAISING FROM PHILANTHROPIC FOUNDATIONS

In addition to donations that can be raised from private individuals, it is possible and even vital to contact foundations and commercial businesses with donation requests. Foundations and firms often have different interests than those of private individuals, but many of the important principles of fundraising from organizations are the same. Thorough preparation, attention to detail, and a personal connection are still the fundamentals.

When raising funds from philanthropic foundations, it's important to examine the interests and needs of the foundations themselves. For example, a foundation often needs to donate a certain percentage of its assets. If the foundation owns assets with a total value of $100 million, and its articles or the tax laws require it to contribute 5 percent of its assets each year, it has to donate $5 million a year. In other words, just as the fundraiser needs to raise money, sometimes the donor has to give away money. When I sat down to lunch in Cleveland one day with my friend Lee Kohrman, president of the David and Inez Myers Foundation, and I began to clear my throat and prepare to ask for a donation, he cut me off playfully and said, "Go on, Sagi. Don't feel embarrassed. I need to give just like you need to fundraise. We're just doing our jobs."

There are many philanthropic foundations, but even more organizations that would like to receive a donation from those foundations. How can we know which foundation might donate specifically to our organization? Here are a few basic rules:

- **Research the foundation's mission and mandate.** Most of the time, this information is available on the foundation's website. Foundation guides supply information about a large number of foundations, in which it is possible to learn the purpose of each. Foundations might focus on economic development in poor cities, equal opportunity for minorities, high school education, immigrant rights, environmental awareness, scientific research, and hundreds of other areas. If your organization's activities (or a specific project at the organization) clearly match the defined purpose of the foundation, that's wonderful. But even when they do not match, there may be other conditions (a personal connection, freedom of board members to give as they please, causes not listed in the organization's official literature, etc.), and you need not give up on the possibility of receiving support from that foundation.

- **Make a personal connection with the management of the foundation.** People give to people. Check out the professionals managing the foundation (CEO, program manager) and the volunteer leadership of the foundation (chairman, president, board members). A personal connection with one of them is an excellent way to start examining the possibility of support from that foundation. This does not mean that being a friend of a senior member of the foundation ensures receiving their support. However, it definitely will help you get their attention and ensure that your proposal is reviewed properly, which is sometimes difficult to achieve through the official channels alone.

- **Check the foundation's giving history.** If the foundation donates significant amounts to organizations similar to your own or located in the same geographic region as yours, take it as an encouraging sign. However, if the foundation only donates to large organizations, for example, and you manage a small nonprofit, that's not a very encouraging sign.

How Should You Contact a Foundation?

Ascertain the correct mode of contact. Foundations that permit applications (some don't even accept unsolicited proposals) prefer different modes of contact. There are foundations that ask for a letter of intent (LOI) to be provided in writing so that they can determine whether supporting the organization is even relevant to their foundation. There are foundations that ask for a full proposal to be submitted according to certain rules or in a specified format. There are also foundations (albeit not many) that will accept phone inquiries. Some foundations can only be contacted online. Some foundations have consultants for various matters through whom contact must be made.

When your connections and network permit it, we recommend beginning a relationship with a foundation by scheduling a meeting, or at least a phone conversation, with the person who makes the decisions. This allows you to formulate your proposal according to the foundation's needs and beliefs, with a better understanding of their interests and preferences. It will also help you connect your organization's activities to their expectations, and most of all – determine whether to even apply to the foundation at all, or if the attempt will be a mutual waste of time. There's nothing that can top a personal connection. Your connection could become your advocate inside the foundation if a process indeed begins to develop.

Some fundraisers try to bypass the professionals at philanthropic foundations and contact the donor – the founder of the foundation – directly. This could be a grave mistake, as K., a senior executive at one of the large family foundations in the United States, once explained to me:

> Many people think that the professional working at the foundation is an obstacle on the path to their long-awaited donation. They prefer to try to bypass them and get to the donor directly. Working like this is liable to

be met with a cold shoulder from the donor, who feels that his representative has been skipped over. In addition, the professional at the foundation could have helped the fundraiser with his application and showed him how to submit the material in the best possible manner.

Timing. As in most other areas in life, in fundraising – and especially when dealing with foundations – good timing is a very important factor for success. One day, I received a call from my friend Eitan Gedalizon, CEO of Tel Hai College, for which I was fundraising at the time. He had heard about a large foundation that invests in higher education. "I made a few phone calls and scheduled a meeting for us with the executive director of the foundation," he said. A few days later, we met with the foundation's executive director at her office at Caesarea's ancient port. The meeting was friendly, there was chemistry between us, and when it ended, the foundation manager told us that we had come at a great time – the foundation had just decided to invest in scholarships for higher education. She instructed us to submit a request for 1.5 million dollars for scholarships. We walked out of the meeting, looked at each other and said, "Let's go out for ice cream!" It seemed too good to be true for a first meeting.

A few weeks later, we were notified that the foundation had approved a donation of 1.5 million dollars to the college, spread out over three years. Later, the foundation expanded the scope of its operations and donated to the college for many more years. Stories like this one do happen, but not very often. Our stars were aligned: the cause fit their purpose, their giving capabilities matched our need, and the timing was perfect. I have enjoyed excellent personal relationships with the leadership of some foundations, but if the timing was no longer right and they had changed the focus of their operations, no donations resulted from those relationships.

A warm contact is better than a cold letter. Some people recommend sending grant proposals to as many foundations as possible, hoping that the quantity will produce results. This approach has its advantages, because it's often difficult to know which foundation will ultimately contribute to your organization, and logically, the more you try, the better chance you have to succeed. But I prefer a more focused approach. This is especially true when the donations are being raised for small or medium-sized organizations, which usually have time and personnel limitations; these resources must be utilized effi ciently. Therefore, it is recommended to start a relationship with a foundation through a specific person, and not with a cold-call letter or written request.

The personal connection could be the foundation's representative, man- ager of the relevant programs at the foundation, or the foundation director him- or herself. But it is always best to contact someone you know personally or with whom you share a mutual friend or colleague. In order to find out who could make the introduction for you, it's a good idea to check online for a list of the members of the management team, the advisory board, and the board of directors. Try to find someone with whom you have a personal con- nection, who can open the first door for you. After a few years in fundraising, you can almost always find "someone who knows someone."

When the initial contact is made in a personal manner, the chances of receiving a useful and direct answer are much higher. Added benefits are obtaining an updated and detailed picture of the causes the foundation supports and learning the best way to present and submit your grant pro- posal. Information that can't always be found in the official sources might be divulged, such as who really decides whether the donation should be given, which buzzwords should be put into the proposal, and ways of lobbying for your organization (or not).

Bettering Your Odds

Understand the foundation's interests and system. Foundations usually have defined areas of focus. It is not always easy for the foundation's manage- ment or owner to locate organizations whose activities, target audience, and strengths successfully match the sector the foundation is interested in sup- porting. An organization that meets these criteria, especially in niche areas (with few active players), has an advantage from the get-go and a good chance of receiving support.

Strengthening and backing a proposal sent to a foundation. You've discov- ered a foundation that could potentially support your organization. You checked that the foundation supports your areas of operation. You prepared and submit- ted a grant proposal. Now what? Philanthropic foundations are made up of peo- ple, too. The decisions are made by people, not just a sophisticated computer that checks all the proposals and determines mathematically which program or project is the most important and worthy of the foundation's support.

Human decision makers are subject to influence. I don't recommend calling the foundation manager every morning and reminding him or her that your organization is the best. Don't ask every person who knows someone at the foundation to pressure them to approve your request, either. But sometimes, a modest phone call to a decision maker with whom you are friendly or a board member you know, saying that you submitted a proposal for a certain project, could help get the document picked up from the bottom of a pile of hundreds of proposals. This will ensure that someone reads it with interest and personal attention.

You can also strengthen your proposal in a more indirect manner. For example, after you've submitted the proposal to the foundation, you can send your contact person a positive article from the newspaper about the project for which you are seeking funding, showing its wonderful impact on the community and the importance of expanding its reach to additional communities.

Information sources regarding foundations. There are many sources that can be used to identify foundations, including the internet, services provided by consulting companies that specialize in researching foundations and preparing grant proposals for submission, and of course, word of mouth. The challenge is to find the foundations that are a good match for your organization and identify an appropriate contact person with whom to begin a relationship. In Israel, a body called the Foundations Forum is made up of members who are representatives or managers of foundations active in Israel. Its purpose is to facilitate the exchange of information, coordination, planning, mutual enrichment, and networking. The forum guards the details of its members zealously. Anyone involved in fundraising is prohibited from coming within a ten-mile radius of their meetings. A fundraiser who manages to obtain the list of members of the forum, their contact information, and the areas of activity of each foundation has an excellent starting point to collect the relevant information about foundations in Israel and their contributions. In the United States, one may seek information about foundations from sites such as Candid, Nonprofit Explorer, and others (Charity Watch is a useful source of information as well).

Hosting foundation representatives. Site visits are the best opportunity to impress foundation representatives and recruit them for your organization. The wise have already said that seeing is better than hearing, which is why one hour of a successful visit at your organization, meeting with the staff, volunteers, and/or those benefiting from the donations is worth much more than several dozen documents and phone calls.

Using a grant writer. Preparing grant proposals is a profession. Not everyone can do it well. I have occasionally encountered organizations who, due to a lack of awareness or in an attempt to cut costs, have just appointed one of the employees at the organization to write the grant proposals. This almost never succeeds. The philanthropic world used to be much more tolerant of a lack of professionalism and a more casual style. But today, grant proposals are expected to be polished and professional. They must provide the information that was requested, explain thoroughly and in detail, but also refrain from being superfluous and exhausting. They must be structured logically, tier upon tier, and maintain a smooth flow and continuum of information. Of course, they must also be written using proper language, grammar, and professional jargon.

After You Apply
What happens when you're rejected? Never burn bridges and don't be disrespectful or aggressive just because you received a negative answer to your proposal. Even if you think that you were the victim of an unfair process, that those who were less deserving got more than you, or that someone specifically tried to harm you or your organization, just don't do it. Aside from the fact that this is poor sportsmanship and disrespectful, it's also a bad way to further your goals. Life flows in a circular manner. When one door is shut, another one opens. Sometimes, it's even the same door, just at a different time. Always respond to rejection by a foundation (or from any donor) in a positive, pleasant manner, thanking them for considering your proposal and giving it their attention. Today the answer is no, but tomorrow it might be yes. Furthermore, the foundation manager who said no today could be the representative of a different foundation that you may contact in the future.

The answer is yes – now develop and cultivate the relationship. You were given a positive answer by a foundation, informing you that the foundation will support your request (even if not for the full amount that you requested). Now is the time to shift gears and strengthen your relationship with the foundation. Write a nice thank-you letter, submit professional reports on time, make sure to update the foundation manager or the relevant contact person about the organization's activities and achievements, invite them to visit, and make sure that whatever you promised would happen does actually happen. Remember: this is just the beginning. A trustworthy, professional relationship will yield results and more support, and the people at the foundation will become your organization's ambassadors and help you recruit additional supporters. It's important to remember that you are not the only one who has fundraising interests and goals to meet. The foundation and its managers have them too. Make an effort to understand their interests, learn what you can do to cater to these interests, and act accordingly.

Periodic reports. Some foundations have a rigid submission format that dictates what and when to report to them. Other foundations leave this to the organization to decide. Make sure to submit the required reports correctly and on time. Put in effort and exercise creativity to prepare reports that are comprehensive but not too long (because who has the patience to read excessive text?). Try to make your reports unique and compelling.

FUNDRAISING FROM BUSINESS CORPORATIONS

The following story is an example of corporate responsibility, sharpness, kindheartedness, and morals. I heard it from my friend Gilad Maoz, a partner at ERM, a leading law firm in Tel Aviv. Gilad told me that a recruitment agency sent him the resume of a candidate for the position of secretary at his law firm. At the bottom of the candidate's resume, the agency had added a note of their own: "Ethiopian, a bit plump."

"That made me mad," Gilad said. "What kind of discriminatory racism is that? We never received a note on any other resume about a 'fat Tunisian' or 'skinny American.'

"I called the head of the recruitment agency and made the severity of the matter clear to her," Gilad continued. "When the manager finished explaining and apologizing, I asked her to take her pick: either we would file a lawsuit against them for discrimination based on ethnicity and external appearance, or we could donate the amount of money that we owe the recruitment agency for previous placements to an organization that advances Ethiopian immigrants."

In this way, an important organization that supports immigrants from Ethiopia will benefit from the situation, the recruitment agency will definitely be more careful in the future, and society will perhaps come one step closer to being more tolerant, just, and fair to all.

Gilad's story is a bit unusual, but there are many reasons that companies make philanthropic contributions. The reasons are numerous and diverse: tax considerations, public relations considerations, a commitment or affinity of one of the company's managers toward a certain cause or organization, geographic commitment to their city or community, and more. In recent years, the trend of commercial companies donating to the community has developed significantly and is often referred to as "social responsibility" or "community involvement."

The CEO of a respected company will have a hard time sitting with his fellow CEOs at a conference on social engagement if he has nothing to answer to the question "What does your company do in terms of community involvement?" Today's CEOs share their company's meaningful contributions and enjoy elaborating on how their employees serve meals at a soup kitchen, tutor kids from a poor neighborhood in math, operate a club for teens with special needs that was established thanks to the company's donations, and more.

To Whom Do Companies Donate?

As mentioned, there are many different types of corporate donations. We can divide them into a few groups:

- **Operationally connected donations.** There are companies that prefer to donate to the community in areas in which they have a relative advantage, connected to their business. For example, a software company might want to donate its software to schools or have its employees donate their time tutoring students in computer skills. A real estate company might want to help renovate apartments for needy senior citizens.

- **Geographically connected donations.** Companies active in a specific geographic region may choose to donate to the community living in that area. I once asked a large high-tech company located relatively close to a college to donate money to support the students. Despite reaching the person responsible for the company's donation decisions through a close connection, I was told that the company is committed to strengthening the local community at its location and therefore only donates to organizations based in that city.

- **Preselected thematic donations.** In order to be effective and also transparent when making their decisions, many companies prefer to focus on a certain area or a few areas of activity and only contribute to support them. There are companies that only contribute to the empowerment of women in business, to education, or to food security, for example. Often, large companies choose a specific area of activity each year, publicize it, and choose which causes to support accordingly.

- **In-kind donations.** There are companies, especially smaller ones, that choose not to donate money. Instead, they prefer to contribute activities or valuable assistance that is equal to money. For example, a food company may donate its surplus to a hunger-relief organization, and a company that markets electrical appliances may donate space heaters to the elderly in the winter. A skincare products company may want to donate some of its merchandise to shelters for women and children. Donations of activities can include organizing the company's employees to volunteer as tutors, to build homes, to clean local parks, to teach teens about managing their money, and more. Fundraisers and organization managers are not always appreciative enough of companies who send their employees for educational and volunteer work. The way they see it, it would have been better if the company had donated the monetary value of the hours of work of its employees, or at least contributed to the community in areas in which it truly excels.

- **Personally motivated donations.** A significant part of the company's decision on how to donate to the community depends on the feelings and areas of interest of its owners and managers. A clear example of this is Virgin Unite, whose good works are inspired by its founder, Richard Branson.

Which Companies Might Donate?

Before you contact commercial businesses to fundraise, it is vital to analyze your relative advantages and relevant assets and to evaluate which companies may be interested in donating specifically to your organization. A classic example of this is the assistance that companies provide to help the victims of natural disasters. When Louisiana and Florida and the surrounding states were dealing with humanitarian care and clean-up after Hurricane Katrina in 2005, many US companies decided to help organizations located in or near the affected areas. An organization from New Orleans that asked for assistance during that period had a higher chance of receiving a donation from commercial businesses than a nonprofit from Seattle, Washington, for example.

After the Second Lebanon War, we at Tel Hai College learned that the IDB Group, which was the strongest group of companies in the Israeli market at the time, had decided to invest NIS 100 million (a little under $25 million) to strengthen the Galilee region. We were able to attract the attention of the decision makers in the group with the help of the personal assistant to Chairman Nochi Dankner. We reached the assistant thanks to the chairman of the college's board of trustees, Avraham Shochat, a former Israeli finance minister. After the initial connection was made with IDB, the ball was already in our court, and we became one of the recipients of IDB's investment. A contact person from within the company is often a prerequisite for having a good chance when contacting a business about a donation.

Who Makes the Donation Decisions?

At small- and medium-sized companies, usually it is the CEO or someone on his or her behalf (often the HR manager) who makes the decision about donating to the community. The CEO is sometimes assisted by a committee composed of company employees, while at other times, the process is less formal. At large companies, there is often a specific person or even a small team responsible for community giving. In such cases as well, the CEO and other senior members of the management still have significant weight in the decision-making process. At private companies, the owner plays an important role, both in determining the areas of activity for donations and making the specific decisions regarding who will receive its support.

Each company is a unique organism with its own procedures and structure, and it is important to try to understand them when asking for a donation. When I contacted one of the large food companies in the Israeli market for a donation, I started the process via one of the founders of the concern, despite the fact that he no longer had an official position at the company. After he put in a good word and referred us to the key person we needed to talk to, we received special attention, friendly treatment, and finally even a sizable donation.

How Should You Make Contact?

Contacting a company can be done officially by submitting a formal letter in writing, either by mail or via the company website. Contact can also be made in a less official manner by calling a friend who works at the company and is familiar with the players and the relevant procedures. You can ask for a meeting with the person responsible for community involvement or the CEO, or invite them to visit your organization, or anything else that could facilitate that initial contact and provide an opportunity to examine whether you have shared interests. I prefer the personal touch.

It's a good idea to collect information about the company's involvement in community outreach, organizations that the company has donated to in the past, who makes the donation decisions at the company, and the criteria for donating. With this important information, you can submit a written proposal that is focused and targeted, as opposed to a shot in the dark. For example, when I contacted one of the large banks in Israel to support one of our programs for which I was raising funds, I already knew which areas the bank usually donated to, the important key words to include in my proposal (in this case, it was the words "financial empowerment of women"), what not to write, the specific person to whom to address the proposal, who should receive a copy of the proposal, and so on.

When Is It Better Not to Receive?

There are a few cases in which corporate donations are best avoided. This is true for example when the value of the donation is less than the cost of the preparations and the headache involved in receiving it. I once contacted a company to request support for one of the programs of the college I was representing. The person overseeing donations at that company said that they do not donate money, but could perhaps hire the college's students to tutor schoolchildren in the city where the company is located. I decided that the college students had enough employment opportunities closer to the college. This type of arrangement would involve a significant time investment on my part as well as travel time for the students that was not justified by the minimal benefit the college students would receive.

The second example of donations not worth receiving is when the contributing company's demands are disproportional. I once received an offer of a donation of scholarships from one of the financial institutions in Israel. Then the institution's regional manager hinted to me bluntly, in a manner that left no room for doubt, that he expected us to market his institution's services at the college and even transfer the organization's investments to his institution for management. I decided that with friends like that, it's better not to even start a relationship.

Another example is when the company is interested in donating for an activity that does not exist or is not needed by the organization. The organization does not need to bend over backwards to receive a donation. Contributions are effective and useful when they support the organization's operations and goals and smoothly integrate with their existing work. In other words, when you need to invent a new program that is not in line with the organization's work plan just to receive a donation, the program and the donation are doomed for failure in the long term.

After the Commitment Is Made

This is when the second part of a fundraiser's work begins. First, make sure that the donation indeed arrives as promised. Second, verify and ensure that the program proposed to the contributing company is in fact executed as promised to them. Third, solve any problems and be the connecting link between the donors and the people running the program at the organization. Last but not least, continue to develop the connection with the company and its personnel, so that the donation will be the first of many more – and perhaps even larger – donations in the future.

CHAPTER 8

PUBLICITY AND MARKETING

What are the best ways to use our time and financial resources, and how will the right messages reach the right people in real time?

A newspaper article, television show, mention in a gossip column, YouTube clip, Facebook likes, interview on a radio show…sometimes, it seems that publicity has transformed from a means to a goal in itself. Everyone wants to be famous. But if we isolate our publicity goals from the ever-intensifying human desire to be famous, we will see that there are several reasons to advertise a nonprofit's activities:

1. Publicity makes more people aware of the organization's work, giving them a chance to join in, support, and assist it.
2. Publicity (positive, of course) enables existing supporters of the organization to feel good about their support.
3. Publicity (positive, of course) can lead potential supporters to decide to support the organization.

When he was about twelve years old, my eldest son Guy told me that he had decided to donate money to an organization that takes care of abandoned dogs. When I asked why he chose specifically this organization, he replied that he heard about them on the radio and was impressed by their work. The organization earned itself a young donor thanks to its publicity work.

USING THE MEDIA

What Is Dangerous about Exposure?

Media advertising is a double-edged sword. It can build your reputation or trash it. There are plenty of examples that demonstrate this, in various contexts. Almost every organization has sides that it would like to expose to the public and aspects that it would prefer to keep quiet. When the media spotlight focuses on you, you don't always have control over what it will shed light on, what will interest the media, what will be correctly understood and what will be taken out of context. There are those who claim that "there's no such thing as bad publicity," but I'm not so sure about that in our context. Without getting into details, it is important to remember that not all publicity serves the organization's fundraising goals or strengthens the fundraiser's position with the organization and its donors.

Who Needs to Be at the Forefront?

When we established the new campus of Tel Hai College at the foot of Mount Hermon, we benefited from close collaboration with the staff of Israel's President Shimon Peres. One day, I visited my friend Efrat Duvdevani, Chief of Staff of the President's Office, to show her photos of the progress of our campus construction. Efrat was excited to see them and said, "Wait here a minute, I'd like you to come in and show the photos to the president." About half an hour later, I entered the office of Israel's president, without any prior planning, and shared with Peres the progress of the establishment of the new campus in the Upper Galilee.

I left the president's residence excited and with great photos of myself showing our activities to the president. I contemplated what I should do with the photos. In the end, I decided that the only people I would show them to would be my own family. Why? After all, we could have sent the photos to our organization's donors. I chose not to publicize the photos because I thought that a meeting with the president of Israel should be attended by the president of the organization and the chairman of its board of governors, not just the organization's vice president (myself). I thought that while publicizing the photos might win me and the organization a few credit points with the donors, it could also harm my personal relationship with the college president.

In contrast, at another organization where I was a board member, the CEO published an attractive brochure in which he was the star of most of the photos. Needless to say, the chairman of the organization wasn't too pleased with the publication, which was perhaps one of the factors that contributed to the CEO's dismissal six months later.

ADVERTISING – WHEN AND HOW

Aside from the inherent dangers of advertising, there is usually a significant cost involved. It is not cheap to advertise an organization on various media channels, and the monetary investment isn't always justified by the results. Advertising can be a financial burden, especially for small organizations. When is it worth the expense? Here's an example. During the Second Lebanon War in the summer of 2006, I understood that this was an opportunity for Tel Hai College. The college is located in the Upper Galilee, in the heart of the area hit by thousands of rockets. After consulting with my colleagues, we decided on the tag line "Despite and Because" (of the bombing) as our slogan. We purchased advertising space in print media. It cost us tens of thousands of dollars, an unprecedented expense for the fundraising budget of a medium-sized organization in the Galilee. But the timing was crucial, because during those weeks, the world's eyes were focused on our region – a once-in-a-lifetime opportunity. Indeed, after the war, we raised tens of millions of dollars, an all-time high, which we used to build the campus, dormitories, provide scholarships, and develop new programs.

First of all, the question of where to advertise is connected to the question of where your potential donors can be found. Assuming that the organization's advertising budget is limited, as well as the organization's time resources for working on free publicity (such as social media posts or interviews on media channels), the management must ask itself: What are the best ways to use our time and financial resources, and how will the right messages reach the right people in real time?

In local news outlets, there are often invitation-style advertisements or announcements of conferences, seminars, or symposiums held by various organizations. This is an example of an advertisement that looks like an invitation to an event but is more importantly a means of publicly announcing the existence and work of the organization. In printed newspapers, it is sometimes possible to arrange news coverage related to a paid advertisement. In other words, buy an ad in our newspaper, and we'll write a supportive article about you. In advertising magazines, such as the airline magazines distributed in the back pocket of the seats on flights, this is obvious. Almost every article about a destination, food, shopping venue, or arts and entertainment is connected to one of the paid ads in the magazine. Is this ethical and right? We won't be the judge of that here. But paid advertising is becoming less and less central in the advertising world. Companies and organizations are realizing that the best publicity for them is the unpaid kind: word of mouth, social media, good deeds, original work, giving awards and certificates of appreciation, involving the public in their activities, and most of all, being professional, trustworthy, sustainable, innovative, and relevant.

MARKETING MATERIALS

Most fundraising work is essentially the transmission of messages – written and oral. Creative, rich writing is vital to fundraising work. Writing comes into play in preparing marketing materials, writing proposals and thank-you letters, personal correspondence and keeping in touch with donors, scheduling meetings, email correspondence, and communication with traditional media outlets. In other words, in almost every field and outlet. The ability to distill a project, need, activity, or vision into a written narrative that is rich, exciting, and comprehensive – yet still succinct and focused – is critical for fundraising work. The secret of good writing is a combination of art and technique. Skilled writers touch upon emotion and intellect, keeping to the minimum necessary length while displaying sensitivity to the nuances of the words. What's more, they avoid potential pitfalls (of course, no one is immune to making mistakes).

The marketing world is broad and innovative. The sky's the limit in terms of ways of marketing the organization's messages to existing and potential donors. But what are the marketing materials that every nonprofit organization should have? A basic list follows.

Website

A website (and a social media presence, at least a passive one) is the showcase of every organization. Someone who hears about an organization and wants to know more should be able to go to the website at any time, anywhere in the world, and read what that organization says about itself. Therefore, every organization, even the smallest and newest ones, needs a professional, attractive, and updated online presence where anyone can get the latest news about its work and contact a representative. A nonprofit that has a global presence should also consider translating its website, or at least preparing a few basic landing pages in other languages. In addition, make sure the website reads smoothly on a cell phone.

Promotional Brochure

Despite today's extensive digitization and the fact that almost everyone can check the organization's website and get other information from the internet, I still believe in the importance of giving donors promotional material printed on actual paper, which they can hold in their hands. Digital material is easily deleted and disappears into the digital black hole. Paper, especially when it's high quality, is harder to throw in the trash. I once came to the office of a big donor in Toronto. During the conversation, I suddenly noticed the promotional brochure that I'd given him a year earlier on his desk next to other marketing materials. From the way it was placed on the table, it was clear that the donor hadn't taken it out in honor of my visit – it had simply stayed there for a full year. This was a sign of the success of the brochure. It had fulfilled its purpose. A promotional booklet is also a physical presence that stays with the donor: it serves as a reminder for the donor after the meeting is over to consider, decide, and let us know about a donation.

In order to fulfill its purpose, a promotional booklet must be:

- **Polished.** Nicely designed, printed on quality paper (but not necessarily expensive), big enough to have appropriate presence.
- **Professional.** Well written, without spelling mistakes and using professional, correct language.
- **Graphically pleasing.** Not too crowded with text, characterized by a good balance of text, photos, empty space, colors, and fonts.
- **Appropriate.** Designed in a manner that fits the organization and its character.

- **Focused.** A promotional booklet does not need to tell all the stories and details of the organization. It needs to tell the main points and core elements and leave the reader curious to learn more about the organization and its work.

Project Proposals

The purpose of a project proposal or giving opportunity is to explain why you need the donation and to display the organization's priorities and development plans. Sometimes, they can also be adapted to the potential donor's areas of interest. I have encountered nonprofits that were interested in raising money but couldn't provide a concrete, reliable answer to the question "What do you need this donation for?"

It is recommended to leave a specific donation request in the hands of the donor. It is easy to get confused when meeting with a donor who is excited by your story and shows empathy and interest in helping you. He keeps saying how important your work is and even promises to consider donating. But a few minutes after the meeting is over, his head and his time are already filled with a thousand other matters. Even if he considered donating during your meeting, that nice thought may be pushed to the back of his mind. Be sure to leave a document that describes the importance of the organization or the project. It must be written succinctly, professionally, and in positive, exciting terms. That way, you leave a reminder of your meeting and increase your chances that the empathy and moral support will be translated into a monetary donation.

The donation request document has many names – giving opportunity, sponsorship request, donation or grant proposal. Yet it has one purpose – to present to a potential donor, in writing, in a clear and comprehensive manner, what is being requested, why, how much, when, and how.

The donation request can be addressed to a specific donor, corporation, or foundation, in which case it is best to write the name of the person or entity at the top of the proposal. It can also be a general request that may be sent to anyone.

The proposal can be written in response to a request for proposal (RFP) by a foundation or donor, or as an uninvited initiative. The proposal can be written according to the donor's guidelines or any way that the writer chooses.

Only someone who has been on the other side, among those whose job it is to read, analyze, and evaluate proposals, can truly understand the importance of succinct, focused writing in a proposal. In short, a donation proposal (like most other documents) must contain everything that needs to be included, but *only* what needs to be there. Do a favor to yourself and the donor or his or her representatives – don't be redundant. Don't try to write all the information that exists about the organization or the program. Focus on what is important and relevant. It's not easy.

An American donor from the venture capital world once explained to me how pricing works when making a promotional video for an organization or company. Anyone can make a twenty-minute video with a video camera that costs $500. But to make a five-minute video, you need a professional, and that will cost at least $5,000. To produce a one-minute promotional video is literally an art, and it'll cost at least $20,000. The same is true of proposals: anyone can write a five-page proposal. But writing a clear, compelling one-page proposal – that's an art.

Guidelines for Preparing a Donation Request

A donation request usually must include seven primary elements that answer the following guiding questions:

- **What's the bottom line?** A summary of the proposal (in the business world, this is called the executive summary). This one- or two-paragraph section tells the reader what you are asking for. The reader will then either continue to read the details of the proposal, stop after the summary, or skim the remainder of the document.
- **Who are we?** Background about the organization asking for the donation: its vision, objective, what makes it unique, and who its leadership is.
- **What is the program?** What do you want to do? What are the objectives of the program?
- **How will the program operate?** What is the plan of action for reaching the program's objectives? What is the order of action items? Can it be operated in a modular manner?

- **When?** What is the timeline for implementing the program?
- **How much?** What is the budget for the program? Who are the financing partners? What will happen after the requested financing is used? Who will continue to fund it?
- **How will success be measured?** What are the criteria for evaluating the program? Who will measure them and how?

Newsletters and Reports

The fundraising world is a difficult, constant struggle for the donor's attention in a world overloaded with stimulants. Not every organization can afford itself the luxury of fighting on all media fronts, but in general, a nonprofit wants its existing and potential donors to hear about its work and achievements as much as possible.

Therefore, it is important to send activity updates, reports, success stories, and accounts of events to as large an audience as possible, to the extent that your budget and human resources permit. This can be done via an e-newsletter sent using an email marketing program, through social media networks, or using other media (photos, videos, text, audio, and more). Remember that public reports, such as an email newsletter, are not supposed to replace the personal, focused, and private reports that various donors should be receiving to tell them how their money was used. There is nothing better than a face-to-face meeting, a telephone call, or at least a personal letter sent to the donor to describe how his or her generous contribution was used.

Business Cards

A business card is just a small piece of paper, but it's much more than that. Your card is often the first information (and sometimes the last) that a potential donor or partner receives from you. It also gives you an opportunity to ask for the other person's card in return, which is vital for staying in touch. In addition, it can serve as a reminder that you met the other person, and that reminder should be presentable and convey quality. Therefore, your business card should:

- Include the important information for contacting you, and only that. For example, fax numbers are no longer vital, and including two email addresses takes up too much room.
- Match the design style of the organization's marketing materials and represent the organization's values. For example, if your organization is involved in helping immigrants, you can write the following slogan on the bottom of your card: "Number 1 in Immigration." If it's an educational organization, maybe add a motto like: "Where children are center stage."
- Made of quality paper that doesn't easily crumple or leak ink.
- Written without spelling mistakes. It's best to stick to one language on your card. If you need more than one, you can print two types of cards.

Using Technology

Modern technology allows fundraisers to use a variety of original applications, which are not prohibitively expensive. For example, with a tablet, you can show your donor a video, photos, and your website over lunch. What once necessitated the lugging of projectors and screens can be done today anywhere and for a very low price. Remember, the key to success is not your technological tools, but rather using them wisely and in an original manner.

FUNDRAISING IN TOMORROW'S WORLD

The speed at which our world changes is constantly increasing. The difference between today's reality and one generation ago is almost beyond comprehension. We can hardly imagine what it was like pre-internet, smartphones, navigation apps, and email. It's shocking to ponder what the world might look like twenty-five years from now.

Technological changes have an impact on the fundraising world. In the not-so-distant past, communications with donors living far away was done by snail mail. Weeks would pass from the time the letter was sent until it was read. But as I write these words, it's now possible to send thousands of donors photos, videos, audio messages, and more with the click of a mouse. Until recently, the donor was dependent on information received from the organization. Today, however, almost all of the organization's information, activities, budget, and personnel are an open book to anyone who knows where and how to find them. It's also harder for people to conceal information or make it look better.

Soon (since the technology already exists), fundraisers will be able to put virtual reality masks on their potential donors and show them a future reality. The potential donor wearing the mask might see a future gymnasium where children are playing, with her name emblazoned on the building. Or a clean, fully equipped playground that will be built with his assistance.

As in many other areas, the future of fundraising will surely experience surprises and technological innovations. But there is one thing that I believe will not change, at least not in the foreseeable future: the importance of human contact. Although there may be times when circumstances beyond our control will limit us, we should always try as much as possible to look someone in the eyes, hear, and listen. To cultivate the interpersonal relationship. Never underestimate the importance of direct contact between the donor and the fundraiser. This brings us back to the three Rs of fundraising: Relationships, Relationships, Relationships.

CHAPTER 9

WHAT MAKES A GOOD
FUNDRAISING PROFESSIONAL?

The ability to listen is more important than being a talented speaker or presenter.

At one of the academic institutions where I headed resource development, we searched far and wide for a professional to take over fundraising efforts in Israel. After interviewing several candidates, we started to feel frustrated that finding the right person was so difficult. Just then, the answer came from a completely unexpected direction.

One evening, we hosted a couple of friends at our home in Hoshaya. The husband was a retiree of the Mossad, Israel's national intelligence agency. During the course of the evening, he asked me curiously, "Tell me, this fundraising stuff…what exactly do you do and what traits does a successful fundraiser need to have?" As I attempted to answer his question, I saw the wheels turning in his head. "You know," he said, smiling, "the traits you're describing are very similar to the traits for employees at the organization I just retired from…"

At this point, I also started thinking out of the box. The next day, I made a few phone calls and reached the supervisor responsible for placement of retired Mossad agents. I told her what I was looking for. "I think I can help you," she answered excitedly. We met a few days later. She brought along resumes of a few candidates. One of them, a retiree who had served in the Mossad for several decades, had been looking for a second career. She joined my staff a few weeks later.

WHAT ARE THE MAIN TRAITS OF A GOOD FUNDRAISER?
People Skills
Ability to connect with different types of people. Fundraising means meeting, contacting, and motivating people with a very wide range of backgrounds, abilities, and styles. This can include the project manager for whom one is raising the funds, the maintenance worker cleaning the building before donors arrive, and donor representatives. Of course, this also includes the donors themselves, who are often members of the financial and social elite in their communities and countries. A fundraising professional does not usually have the authority to manage colleagues: official authority is not the factor that will help lead and motivate a fundraising staff. Professional, charismatic leadership and the ability to develop healthy, positive connections with each of the diverse personalities a fundraiser comes into contact with is vital.

Today we have amazing technologies for social interaction, tools that seemed like science fiction just twenty years ago, such as Zoom, Facebook, and WhatsApp. But there's still no substitute for human contact. Face-to-face. You and me, opposite each other. Nothing can replace the long flight and personal meeting with the donor. Not even a Zoom or FaceTime remote meeting, although these might be necessary in crisis times, such as the COVID-19 pandemic. At personal meetings, presentations before a foundation's board of directors, gala dinner speeches, or any interaction, the fundraiser can't hide behind a copywriter. He must be capable of saying the right thing at the right time and in the right place. He needs to get people excited when necessary. He has to know how to apply pressure when possible and lay off when appropriate. He also must be able to express empathy when due.

Listening ability. When I asked my friend Ron Solomon, Bar-Ilan University's legendary fundraiser on the West Coast of the USA, to define the most important trait for a fundraising professional, he boiled it down to one word: "Listening. Listening. Listening." The ability to listen is more important than being a talented speaker or presenter. Many fundraisers and organization managers fail here, focusing on how they will present the issue they seek to advance instead of listening closely enough to the messages the donor is relaying to them – verbally and nonverbally.

Persuasiveness. One of my colleagues told me how she prepares to request a large gift. "I run at the gym or jog in the park and repeat the important lines in my pitch over and over. I work on motivating myself and convincing myself with my own explanations. I try to make myself believe that the project I'm presenting is the most important cause in the world." Fundraisers must be able to persuade people to believe in the vision to the extent that they are willing to part with their money for it. You must establish that the cause is worthy, the people working at the organization are deserving of support, the leadership of the organization is sincere and capable of realizing the dream. Most of all, you must convince the potential donor that the person requesting a donation is worthy of receiving it!

Can-Do Personality

Initiative. This includes self-confidence, motivation, and the ability to work independently in uncertain conditions. A fundraising professional's work, especially during the beginning stages, is done under many uncertain conditions. The fundraiser does not always know what resources will be available (budget, personnel, time), nor even whether people, foundations, and companies will actually want to donate to the organization. After all, the product you are "selling" can't be evaluated like a commercial product. It can't be measured monetarily, by time to market, or in comparison with similar products (I will discuss this point at length in the chapter about donation options). Fundraisers must constantly fuel their own engines and motivate themselves. You must believe in yourself and in the causes for which you are fundraising. You must be capable of traveling around the world, alone for extended periods of time, constantly motivating yourself to keep working and achieving. A typical fundraising professional cannot be managed or pushed to achieve just by giving orders, offering monetary goals, or imposing discipline.

Competitiveness and sportsmanship. A fundraiser must have the ability to fall off the horse and get back up again. During one of her fundraising trips to the United States, my wife wasn't having much luck. She had to raise a significant donation in order to receive a matching challenge grant. But time and again she was faced with refusals from the donors she met. After a week of unsuccessful meetings, she called me in a dejected mood. "It's not working," she said. "I don't know what I'm doing wrong."

It was a cold winter. Even going out for a run (which is her usual stress release) was impossible. She had just two days left until her trip was over, and she had to improve her mood to be up for the meetings that were still ahead. To encourage her and help her overcome the temporary crisis, I used the running image: "You run marathons. You know that marathon runners sometimes hit a wall – that point during the run when they feel like they can't run any further. Then they keep going. They push to get over that wall, and then they can finish their race. You've hit a wall now. Push through it and get the job done!" Indeed, at her second-to-last meeting in New York, she was able to raise a donation of $150,000 and came home overjoyed.

A fundraiser must have a sportsman's soul. When a world-class swimmer gets to the Olympics, he exercises, eats right, and puts all his effort into preparing for the fateful competition for the medal. But no matter whether he succeeds or fails, wins the medal or is eliminated during the preliminaries, the day after the Olympics is over, he starts training for the next challenge. The same is true of a fundraiser. She must be willing to work hard to prepare and practice before trying to get that donation. She must dream. If she's successful and the donor comes on board and commits to a large donation, the fundraiser can go celebrate. But the next morning, she'll still be preparing for the next donation request.

A fundraiser who is given a negative answer must be capable of feeling disappointed, even upset, but must also be able to forget about the disappointment the next morning. You've got to plow ahead to what will hopefully be your next success. The ability to take the blow, to fail but then recover and push toward future success, is just as vital to fundraisers as it is to athletes. Another trait that fundraisers and athletes share is their competitiveness. They dream of raising the bar. After I've obtained a large donation, friends have often remarked to me, "Now you can finally take your foot off the gas pedal and relax a bit…" But that's not how it works. A typical fundraiser will never be satisfied with the donations raised so far; you're always striving to raise more.

The truth is that management isn't usually satisfied with what's been raised either. Expectations rise with success – as the saying goes, "Appetite comes with eating." However, it is always best, both for management and fundraisers, to maintain a healthy level of pressure. It's important to preserve the balance between the natural desire to raise the level of expectations ever higher than the donations obtained and the ability to feel satisfied. Management should always congratulate, give positive feedback, and praise the current achievements.

Creativity and thinking outside the box. The world of fundraising is cruelly competitive. Although there are many wealthy people in the world, the number of people vying for their donations is constantly growing, and the skills of the contenders are constantly improving. I once worked with Mati, a leading businessman. We sat in his office in Manhattan. It was late at night, around ten o'clock. We were both tired, and I was already sending signals to the effect of "Let's call it a day and go to sleep." But he called me to the window of his office and pointed to the skyscrapers opposite us. Despite the late hour, many of the windows were still lit up. "See all those offices with lights on, Sagi? We have to compete with all of them, and they're just like us – working hard and trying to succeed!" In order to succeed in the fundraising world, to win the competition for donors' hearts, and especially when fundraising for lesser-known organizations (because fundraising for Harvard and Princeton is a whole different ballgame), we must be creative and think outside the box.

When I arrived at Tel Hai College, the administration's dream was to build a new campus: two additional buildings; a total cost of about 15 million dollars. It didn't take long for me to realize that hundreds of other organizations, no less worthy than ours, were competing for building fund donations. We needed something different. More exciting. Creative. Something no one else could do better than us. That's how we came up with the idea of the Upper Galilee Development Triangle – a collaboration between research organizations, academic institutions, and the start-up industry to develop the northern periphery of the State of Israel, both economically and socially.

The funding needed to realize this exciting vision jumped to $100 million, spread over a decade. But in addition to increasing the donation amount, we weren't just talking about academic buildings. We presented our potential donors an ambitious plan, backed by three successful and well-respected institutions (the college, a research institute, and a technological incubator).

We described the fair and committed partnership between the leadership of the organizations and detailed the achievements already underway. Then, in the summer of 2006, the Second Lebanon War broke out, directing global attention to the Galilee region. This coincidence led to donations totaling tens of millions of dollars. The funds enabled the construction of the eastern campus of Tel Hai College, which stands proudly at the foot of Mount Hermon.

Fundraisers and organization management must plan and implement creative fundraising strategies. Strategies that will express the organization's uniqueness, its strengths and goals, and its members. Strategies attuned to time and place that will set it apart from the competition, attracting positive attention.

Commitment to the cause and enthusiasm. My friend the late Harvey Krueger of New York, a pioneer of investment banking in Israel, served in many public positions, including Chairman of the Boards of Governors of Hebrew University and Tel Aviv University. When I asked him what was the most important trait of a good fundraiser, he said:

> Without being enthusiastic himself, the fundraiser can't excite donors. I understood this when I was asked by an organization I'm involved with to call my friends and invite them to their gala dinner. When a few of my friends responded in the negative, I tried to understand why I wasn't succeeding in bringing them to the event. It was then that I realized: I wasn't too excited about the dinner myself, and I thought it was doomed to fail. When I was feeling ambivalent, of course I wasn't exciting others.

Cultural and Intellectual Assets

Cosmopolitan outlook. An old fundraiser friend once summed up the experience of meeting with donors using the following comparison. "Think about it," he said to me with a grin, "Not only do we ask very busy people [donors] to give us their precious time, we then ask them for money at the end of the meeting and even expect that they'll want to meet us again! A fundraiser's true test, after meeting with a donor and asking for a donation, is whether the donor agrees and is even happy to see you again in the future."

To pass this test, fundraising professionals must be interesting people who know how to hold a conversation, listen to the other person, and keep up-to-date with world events. They should be pleasant, honest, dressed appropriately for the location and situation, and more. Sound like Superman? Sometimes, that's how it feels. One of the most common questions about the dynamics between donors and fundraisers is "What does the donor get out of it?" Or in other words: "It's obvious what you [the fundraiser] get, but how does the donor benefit?"

I used to meet one of my donors in Canada for lunch at the restaurant he owns. Our meetings would always start like this: "So, what questions do you have for me this time?" When I'm fundraising overseas, I always make sure to keep up with current events. I read the news sites and look at the commentaries, too. The people I meet with expect me to update them, to tell them something they don't know, especially something they wouldn't read in the *New York Times* or *London Times*. I try to give them tidbits that they can share with their friends later. "You know, I met with Melamed the other day. He says that…"

Fluency in languages – oral and written. A professional who wants to start conversations, connect with, and convince people to support a cause must be able to speak the potential donor's language fluently. You must speak with intelligence and sensitivity. In the United States, for example, I define this as "the ability to speak American, not simply English." In England, this means understanding the nuances of British humor, or the fact that "center" and "soccer" in America are "centre" and "football" in England. When you finish a meeting with a potential American donor and he accompanies you to the door of his office and says, "Your project is very important – great work – I'm sure you'll succeed in raising the resources you need for it…," you need to be familiar with American conversational culture to realize that he is essentially telling you that there's practically no chance you'll be getting a donation from him.

Most fundraising work is done by getting a message across – in writing and orally. Rich, creative writing is vital in this profession. Writing comes into play when preparing marketing materials, request letters, thank-you letters, and personal correspondence, as well as keeping in touch with donors. We use our writing skills for scheduling meetings and for email and snail mail correspondence. We also write opinion articles and advertisements in newspapers, on social media, and in traditional media channels. In short, writing skills are needed all the time.

The ability to take a project or vision and write about it in a way that is enthusiastic and comprehensive but also succinct and focused is vital for fundraising. The secret of good writing is combining art and technique to touch both the heart and the mind; writing everything that's important but not everything that you can; being sensitive to the nuances of words; and avoiding, as much as possible (though everyone makes mistakes) stepping on land mines. Excellent writing skills, at least in one language, are critical for fundraisers. Additional languages are obviously an advantage.

Integrity and sound ethics. A good reputation is a fundraiser's best resource. No donor will give at the request of a fundraiser whose reputation has been marred. In the fundraising world, it is sometimes tempting to stray from the honest path. Not necessarily by putting something into one's own pocket, but rather, by misrepresentation – for example, incorrect reporting regarding the way donation money was used, or selling the same project or building to several donors. Donors have often shared with me negative experiences they have had with NGOs. The truth is that the negative experiences aren't always due to improper intentions. A sign on a dedicated building, for example, may fall down or fade and not be replaced out of simple inattention. But if the donor visits and finds the sign missing, extensive efforts will be necessary to restore trust in the organization and its representatives.

The person responsible for fundraising at the organization often feels like a watchdog, protecting the commitments and interests of the donors. I have had to fight with management several times to fulfill promises to donors – whether it's keeping to the schedule, hanging signs, use of donation money, or providing reports. A fundraiser needs to be the donors' representative at the recipient organization. Like it or not, donors view you, the fundraiser, as their representative. They made their commitment to you, and you owe them your commitment.

Problem-solving ability. During one of my trips to the United States, I went out to dinner with Z., a longtime donor, and a few of his friends. Z. was not feeling well that day, and despite the many medications he was taking, he couldn't resist and had a few drinks. On the way back from the restaurant, I offered to take the wheel for him. He refused. I hoped that his alcohol tolerance and the short trip back to his home would make the ride bearable. In hindsight, I regretted it. During the ride, it was evident that he was not alert enough. His wife, who sat behind him, also asked to drive instead of him. He refused this as well and quipped, "Sagi, don't get married [he apparently forgot that I am married with four children]! Marriage only brings trouble…" He continued to drive slowly, threatening all the lampposts on the way. Mercifully, we finally reached his house safely. At this point, Z. was having trouble getting out of the car, and we barely managed to help him into the house. The next day, I called to ask how he was doing, and he didn't remember a thing. In cases like these (and worse), a fundraiser encounters challenges for which no university could prepare him.

SELF-MANAGEMENT

As a fundraiser, you must always remember that you are the primary and most important resource of the fundraising system you represent. You are more important than slideshow presentations, marketing booklets, websites, letters, and video clips. Furthermore, as the Jewish Sages state in *Ethics of the Fathers*: "A good name is better than fine oil," and this holds true for a fundraiser. Your good name, your reputation, your physical and digital presence, and your physical and mental capabilities are extremely vital to your ability to complete your tasks and succeed in the competitive, demanding world of fundraising. The following are a few constant musts for a professional fundraiser.

Network
Stay up-to-date. As in other areas such as business development, marketing, headhunting, and more, a fundraiser must be connected and up-to-date. A lot of information changes hands and a lot of connections, referrals, and introductions take place in less formal situations: at conferences, conventions, and other events. A fundraiser needs to be there, meet people, and be a known figure. Moreover, the philanthropic world, like other worlds of content in the twenty-first century, is a dynamic, ever-changing place. The manager of a museum today will be tomorrow's manager of a philanthropic foundation.

Today's fundraiser will be a donor representative tomorrow, and so on. The connections, the friendships, the ability to assist others and also be assisted by them when necessary, are vital assets to any fundraiser.

Participate in conferences and continuing education. Participation in conferences and continuing education programs is important for a few reasons. The first is that we all can learn and improve, even the most professional people. It is always good to enrich your knowledge, develop in new directions, and be exposed to different opinions, techniques, and new methods in your profession.

Secondly, conferences and conventions are the best places to have meetings, introduce yourself to new people, and renew old connections. The secret that everyone already knows is that in conferences, the important work doesn't happen in lecture rooms and presentation halls. The real stuff happens in the hallways, at coffee breaks, outside of the halls and the lectures. It's the small talk, exchanges of business cards, the whispering, and the updates and exchange of information where the real business happens. So it's important to be there.

Thirdly, a fundraiser should make an effort to be seen. For years, I would faithfully attend the Herzliya Conference hosted by IDC Herzliya. During its early years, it was the most prestigious conference in Israel. Many of the big names from the defense, economic, political, and media echelons of Israel would roam the halls of that conference. I found myself meeting many of them every year at the IDC conference. These encounters led to conversations, which led to connections, which sometimes led to fundraising work. My presence at this prestigious conference was part of my effort to build my brand and the image of the organizations that I represented during those years.

Be Ready and Willing

Always be prepared to meet a donor. I was once asked to help the son of the representative of an Israeli organization find work in Israel after several years of working abroad. I met him at my office. My impression was that he was talented, motivated, and capable, but he showed up to the meeting in clothes that one might wear when running to the corner store, not to a job interview.

At the end of our meeting, I asked him if I could give him some slightly direct personal feedback. He consented. "Listen," I said to him delicately, "when you meet with people who are supposed to be helping you find work, you need to treat any such meeting as if it was a job interview with a potential employer. What you are wearing is probably not what you would wear to an interview. Try to prepare for every meeting as if it was an interview. You never know when and where luck will strike." The same holds true for a fundraiser. When participating in a conference, going out to an event, to an exhibition opening, a professional convention, or anywhere you might meet colleagues, partners, or potential donors, dress accordingly. You never know when and where your good fundraising luck will strike.

Donate yourself. If you don't believe in your organization enough to donate even a symbolic sum to it, how can you expect others to do so? Throughout the years, I always made sure to donate to the organizations where I worked. Where possible (and there were of course places that looked at me as if I had lost my mind), I tried to encourage a giving culture among the other senior management of the organization as well.

Cultivate Mental Fortitude

"When you go to fundraise, prepare two pockets: one pocket for money, and the other pocket for insults," a smart man once quipped. The truth is that it isn't easy to raise money, from a mental perspective. There are often situations where the potential for insult exists. This is built into the role of asking people for their money without offering something tangible in return. What protects a fundraiser from being hurt by potential insults is a state of mind regarding the role and its inherent challenges.

I once met a donor in Beverly Hills, California. The meeting had been scheduled a few months earlier, and I expected to leave it with a significant donation in hand. When I arrived for the meeting with the donor, a man in his eighties, I had to wait for an extended period of time in the waiting room to his office. When the secretary finally showed me in, I was met by impatient, aggressive behavior on his part: "What do you want from me? I'm busy! I only have a few minutes! Every day, fundraisers like you come to see me!" I refused to be intimidated. In a quiet tone, I asked the donor to give me three minutes of his time. He took a deep breath and sat down. Briefly and concisely, I explained to him the purpose of my visit, mentioned the mutual friend who recommended that I meet him, and detailed what was special about the project I was asking him to support. I showed him photos of the project too. The restless donor sat back in his armchair and called over his grandson, who was in the adjacent office. "Come and listen to what this young man from Israel has to share with us." Three minutes became thirty, and at the end, I left the meeting with a sizable donation and a satisfied, happy donor.

Fundraising can take a mental toll. A fundraiser has to ask for money from people and deal with rejections, which are usually more frequent than affirmative answers. It involves exhausting travel around the world and work that is usually done alone and far away from family and colleagues. You must meet rigid objectives that are constantly increasing, while the needs are always greater than the resources. What's more, managers and colleagues often show a lack of understanding regarding the essence and nature of fundraising work in general. All this can decrease morale and cause burnout. But there is a solution to this problem. The solution can come from several directions:

1. Mental fortitude can come from within. A fundraiser must constantly remind herself and be capable of internalizing the essence and purpose of her work: "To cause and enable good people with means to do good deeds and make the world a better place." Internalizing this statement makes it a lot easier to deal with insults and frustration.
2. Outside support can help too. A manager who is smart enough and sensitive enough knows when to throw in a kind word, when to encourage, when to pat on the back, and when to find original ways of rewarding the fundraiser on his bumpy road. A kind word is often worth much more than a monetary prize.
3. Donors can be a source of energy for fundraisers as well. Meetings with donors, who are usually among some of the most talented, sharp, and successful people in the world, can give fundraisers the motivation and energy boost to keep going. A good fundraiser knows how to derive mental strength and recharge her batteries from her donors too – from those good people whom she has convinced to make the world a better place.

Manage Your Reputation

Enhance your digital presence. Having a digital presence is becoming more and more important to a professional's status and networking efforts. This includes a profile on social media platforms such as Facebook and LinkedIn, managing the frequency and context of search engine results for your name, and publishing professional articles in your field. But your digital presence can be a double-edged sword too. In the event that a potential donor searches for your name online (and they do), even on a non-professional social media platform, and finds an embarrassing and unflattering post from years ago, it probably won't encourage the donor to contribute to you and the organization that you represent. A fundraiser should always be presentable, respectable, and respectful, and should make sure that tone is reflected in his or her online presence.

Guard your good name. Most importantly, watch your reputation! At the end of the day, after all is said and done, your reputation is your most valuable asset. A fundraiser whose name precedes her as someone who is not trustworthy, who makes promises but doesn't keep them, who is unprofessional, or even indirect or vague, should find herself another profession. In contrast, a fundraiser who embodies those elements that make a fundraiser successful and loved by others will benefit significantly from her stellar reputation. The donors she meets and recruits along the way will walk alongside her, back her up, and act on her behalf.

COMPETITION IN THE FUNDRAISING WORLD

My wife and I worked in fundraising for nonprofits for many years and still do. We have each raised and continue to raise money for different organizations over time. We have both been asked dozens of times by friends and colleagues about competition between us. "Do you compete for donors?" The answer was always the same: "There is no competition, and there doesn't need to be. There are enough donors to go around." Of course there is a sense of competitiveness among organizations, among the leaders of organizations and their fundraisers. There is struggle among egos, a competition over who is most successful. That always exists, not necessarily in the context of donations. But most of the time, the competition is not over donors, but rather concerning the ability to raise funds in general.

When I managed the fundraising operation for Tel Hai College, I was contacted by a longtime donor and friend in Canada who told me that a large donor was searching for an academic institution for the purpose of giving a strategic donation. My friend introduced me to the potential donor, and at his request, I sent him material about the college and told him about our various development plans. In the end, the donor decided to contribute tens of millions of dollars to the Technion in Haifa instead. Indeed, there had been covert, indirect competition between the Technion and our school, and in this competition, the Technion won. Its characteristics, size, reputation, and areas of specialization were better suited to this donor. Over the strategic donations of millions and tens of millions, there is in fact competition.

Most donors will not parcel out many donations in the tens of millions. They will choose one or two organizations and invest in them, help them grow, become part of their leadership, and see their names proudly displayed on their buildings. But most organization managers and board members reading this book would be happy with five- and six-figure donations too. Donors in this more modest bracket usually contribute to a number of organizations, sometimes even quite a few. In these cases, the competition is not among the organizations, but is instead internal: Are you (your organization, the CEO, the fundraiser) good enough, exciting enough, and successful enough at making connections to be worthy of receiving the attention and contribution of the donor?

Who Is Your Competition?

I have often been asked by donors: "Why should I give to you and not to the X organization, which is involved in similar work?" I never speak badly of another organization. It is a grave mistake (in life in general) to put down another organization or another person to try to make yourself look better. A typical answer to the question of "Why should I donate specifically to you?" could be: "X is a worthy, important organization. I asked for your time to show you why our work is unique, how it is groundbreaking/changes people's lives/enables the creation of opportunities. Your investment in our work will enable us to…" In other words, concentrate on why you are good, and not whether or how a different organization is less so.

To do this well, organization managers and fundraisers need to sharpen and polish the message of the organization (see previous chapters). How is the organization unique? What is the purpose of our activities? What do we do best? What are the results of our work? How might the world/country/neighborhood look without us? How will it look if we double our reach?

In order to succeed in the competitive world of fundraising, as in many other fields, three main components are necessary: ability, hard work, and luck. Ability can always be improved and honed. Hard work must also be focused, to the point, and methodical. As for luck, it's important to be sensitive to it and identify opportunity when it knocks, but again, the focus of your competition is internal – compared with your own achievements and not those of others.

Look for the Blue Ocean

One of my friends, a professor at a leading university, once asked me: "What characterizes your donors?" The question was asked during a period when I led the establishment of a fundraising operation for an academic institution in northern Israel. It was my second such effort. At first, I had a hard time characterizing the donors that I had recruited to support the organization. They seemed so different from each other. They came from different countries, religions, and backgrounds. But when I told my friend about a few of them, he smiled and said, "There's a common denominator. Many of them are not the usual donor; they're off the beaten track and atypical." When I thought about it later, I realized that my friend was right – many of the donors did diverge from the rest of the philanthropic community. There was a reason for that. I always looked for what can be called "the blue ocean."

This expression is taken from *Blue Ocean Strategy* by Renée Mauborgne and W. Chan Kim (Harvard Business Review, 2005). It explains that traditional businesses compete with each other by improving product specifications or their manufacturing procedures, with the objective of increasing their market share within a certain market segment. The authors describe this strategy metaphorically as the "red ocean" strategy. When competitors try to trump each other by grabbing additional market shares, the market becomes crowded, and anticipated profits and growth potential decrease.

This competition turns the ocean red from the blood of the competitors fighting with each other.

An alternative strategy is the blue ocean strategy. The blue ocean is unconnected to existing markets. Instead, it creates demand and new opportunities where growth potential is obvious. Competitors don't fight by maneuvering with pricing, improving product specifications, or using similar manufacturing processes. Instead, they create products with different characteristics while using organizational structures and manufacturing procedures unique to them. The blue ocean strategy therefore creates an ocean that is clean and free of competition, whereby the company applying this strategy markets to a new target audience, based on a substantial competitive advantage that lasts.

A fundraiser can implement this strategy by looking for untapped donor markets instead of trying to lure established donors away from other projects.

CHAPTER 10

RECRUITING AND HIRING THE FUNDRAISING PROFESSIONAL

The short answer is that there is no such thing as an ideal candidate. The long answer is there are those who have better backgrounds than others, and people who have acquired more promising skills than others.

Even before starting to look for a resource development officer, the organization must ask itself the simple question: Is our organization ready to hire a professional fundraiser? Many CEOs skip straight to more practical questions when recruiting a fundraising professional (What is his background? Who does she know? How much has he raised in the past?) without paying enough attention to fundamental questions for recruiting a fundraising manager.

1. Is the organization financially prepared for this step? As a basic rule and as mentioned above, in establishing a new fundraising system, the organization should be prepared for the fact that during the first year, and often the second as well, the fundraising salary and activities will exceed income from additional donations raised. In other words, for one or two years, the fundraising operations will be costing the organization money, not bringing it in! Therefore, an organization that is incapable of investing the necessary monetary resources to finance fundraising during its establishment stage – from its current budget, savings, or even with a specifically earmarked donation – should not begin this "adventure."

2. Are the expectations of management and the fundraiser synchronized?
A friend who interviewed for a fundraising position at a large organization
asked for my advice. He shared that he was expected to raise several million during his first year of activity. When I asked about the organization's
donation history, he replied that they had almost no regular donors. "Even if
they offer you the position, don't take it!" I warned him. "The management's
expectations are unrealistic. You shouldn't put yourself in a position that is
doomed for failure."

3. Are the basic tools for success in place? To successfully fundraise, a nonprofit must have the basic tools for success. The fundraising professional's
capabilities, experience, connections, and enthusiasm are not enough. After
all, she is raising donations for a specific organization, with a specific agenda,
that was formed to fulfill specific objectives and further its mission. What are
these tools for success? Here are some examples.

- **Operations budget.** A budget– even a modest one – is a must for
  facilitating basic fundraising activities such as preparing quality
  marketing materials, a website, and travel expenses (including overseas if necessary).
- **Programs for which donations can be raised.** Without a concrete
  program, there is no goal to raise donations for. We've all seen our
  fair share of charlatans raising money for causes that didn't even exist.
- **Legal status.** An organization must have a certificate permitting
  them to receive donations and issue tax-deductible receipts in every
  country where fundraising is to take place.

Organizations should attend to the above before attempting to hire a professional fundraiser. Candidates, in turn, should check these and other basic conditions before taking on the responsibility of fundraising for the organization.

HOW TO FIND A FUNDRAISER
I've witnessed the following common method of recruiting a fundraising professional. It goes more or less like this: "Our competitor just got a big donation. You know, we also need someone to fundraise for us. Someone who

speaks well and can also write well. Someone who knows wealthy people… Wait, I know someone… She's really nice. She used to work at the botanical gardens… She probably knows a lot of rich people… Let's ask her if she's interested and what her salary expectations are."

Defining the Position

After deciding that it's time to fundraise, an organization must define a concept of its uniqueness, objectives, development plans, and fundraising goals. This doesn't always happen. But before candidates are interviewed and salaries discussed, another preliminary step should happen. The organization's management should formulate a job description and list the traits they seek in a future fundraiser. What does this mean? The job description should be a succinct list of the various tasks that the chosen person will be expected to perform. The list of traits describes the skills, experience, and characteristics of the person being sought.

Sample Job Description for a Fundraising Director

General

- Prepare work plans for the fundraising department
- Plan and lead strategies to position and brand the organization
- Recruit, train, and manage a staff
- Plan and manage the department's budget
- Represent the department within the organization and to outside parties
- Outline and implement a fundraising-focused culture at the organization
- Develop new, current fundraising plans
- Participate in defining the organization's vision and development goals
- Fundraise!

Interaction with Donors and Foundations

- Create, cultivate, and develop connections with donors
- Prepare project proposals and donation opportunities
- Prepare image and marketing materials

- Write reports and updates for donors and foundations
- Plan and execute fundraising events
- Plan and manage visits of donors and Friends groups
- Operate various media entities to promote the fundraising efforts
- Plan, establish, and manage a database of donors
- Plan and execute overseas fundraising trips
- Ask for the gift!

Working with Volunteer Leadership
- Prepare a plan for recruiting and cultivating a board of directors
- Identify potential candidates to join the Friends group based on certain criteria, and recruit new members
- Cultivate and work with board members on fundraising issues
- Solicit board members

Connection with Other Organizations
- Initiate strategic partnerships with local and foreign organizations to advance the organization's objectives
- Act as liaison with partner organizations for projects and fundraising

Reporting
- Report on an ongoing basis to the president/CEO
- Report periodically to the board/Friends organization

The Ideal Candidate's Traits
- Experience with the fundraising world
- Excellent speaking and writing abilities
- Organizational skills, systematic thinking, attention to detail
- Creativity and enterprising spirit
- Aptitude for working with diverse entities locally and abroad
- Excellent interpersonal and listening skills
- Team-player mentality
- Capacity to hear a no and continue to pursue a yes
- Motivation and hunger for success
- Integrity and credibility
- Willingness to work unconventional hours
- Ability to ask for money

I strongly recommend not to begin recruiting before compiling the job description and profile of required traits. This will also help candidates assess themselves: Am I suited to the position? Do I really want it? Does the job description seem logical and appropriate? A recruitment process that starts by defining the job description and required traits also protects against various politics that come into play, which sometimes make it difficult to choose the best candidate for the job. In this way, each candidate is examined against the professional requirements and her anticipated ability to fulfill them well, regardless of who is pressuring to accept her and why.

Background and Training

Several times, I've been asked by organizations to interview a potential fundraising professional. This was usually after the president/CEO met with the candidate and wanted a professional opinion. The manager often sent the candidate to the interview with me with his own positive assessment: "Seems like a good guy. He's got lots of connections; says he knows a lot of donors. He's sure of himself."

As a seasoned fundraiser, I need only a few targeted questions to separate the wheat from the chaff. For example: "Tell me about the biggest donation you ever raised, and what your part in the fundraising process was." Or: "How many new donors did you bring to the last organization where you worked? What was the total amount of donations you raised during your work there? What were the three largest donations received during the last year that you worked there?" Or: "Out of the donors who contributed during the past three years to the organization where you worked, how many do you think would be willing to consider also donating to the next organization you work for?"

Fundraising is a profession. It's a difficult, complex process and takes time to ripen. Candidates who claim to be able to raise a lot of money in a short time and boast about a broad network of connections all waiting for the chance to donate to the next organization that the fundraiser works for will always raise my suspicions.

So Who Is the Ideal Candidate?

The short answer is that there is no such thing as an ideal candidate. The long answer is there are those who have better backgrounds than others, and people who have acquired more promising skills than others.

A professional who worked in alumni fundraising for a few years at a major university will usually receive better fundraising training than someone who worked in the diplomatic corps or foreign service. Why? Universities are focused on fundraising, with extensive experience in this area. They have organized training systems and employee development programs and are internationally oriented. Diplomats, by contrast, are very talented, but don't necessarily have the fundraising experience and touch. Ex-diplomats may be pleasant conversationalists, familiar with the rules of the big world, but aren't experienced in the art and science of fundraising. Moreover, many envoys who have lived overseas as ambassadors, consuls, or representatives of other well-regarded organizations mistakenly think that the respect they received in those positions expresses a willingness to donate money. They (and any organization that expects quick results from them) are usually in for a surprise and heavy disappointment.

Start-ups and medium-sized organizations interested in establishing new fundraising departments should pay attention to the candidate's history. They should be looking for a professional who has already built a new fundraising operation during her career and proven that she can create it from scratch. Someone who has worked at a large organization (such as a university, museum, or hospital) for all his professional life will be accustomed to working with a staff, support, guidance, a strong network of Friends groups all over the world and extensive organizational politics. He may find it difficult to adapt to a new environment where he is a one-person team who has to do it all, create everything anew, and show donation income at the end of the year.

One of the classic deliberations that the management of a small or medium-sized organization faces when recruiting a fundraiser is weighing the importance of the candidate's experience against his or her potential and enthusiasm. In other words, which is better? A person who brings with her years of fundraising experience but might show signs of burnout, or someone who seems very talented and highly motivated, but lacks practical fundraising experience? There is no simple answer to this dilemma, and a decision should be made on a case-by-case basis.

Tamara Elliott Rogers, who led Harvard University's $9.6 billion campaign as the university's Vice President of Alumni Affairs and Development, identifies the key ingredient for a big gift fundraiser as *judgment*:

In recruiting fundraisers, I often say that I would look for five things:

1. Judgment
2. Judgment
3. Judgment
4. Judgment
5. Energy to act on their judgment

I see judgment as encompassing listening skills, open-mindedness and respect for others, a sense of focus, teamwork, and willingness to ask for advice. Why is judgment so important? Because individual fundraising is not done by formula. In every situation and interaction, there will be judgment calls. I actually cared less about a candidate's years of experience and more about these other qualities – superb fundraisers may come from many varied work backgrounds.

Who Is Not Suitable for the Position?

A few criteria can help the management decide whom to remove from their list of candidates at an early stage of the game.

Integrity. With social media available at your fingertips, the world is a very small place. Everyone knows everyone. A friend told me that while he is meeting with a potential candidate, he sends text messages to contacts the candidate mentions, in order to hear their opinions on the spot. A person with a reputation of being dishonest should not be working at your organization. (Of course, take care not to falsely incriminate the innocent.)

Tenure. When a candidate has switched employers several times and never held a job for more than one or two years, this raises a red flag. In fundraising, connections built and cultivated over long periods of time are key. You don't want to recruit someone who will start forming relationships with your donors and then leave the organization a short time afterward and go somewhere else. Furthermore, someone who has not stayed in fundraising positions for very long at several organizations might have been unable to meet expectations and supply the goods. This could signal a "serial failure."

Chemistry. I believe that a critical part of any interview is determining whether you want to say "Good morning" to this person every day for the next several years. The chemistry that exists – or doesn't exist – between the supervisor and the candidate is an important element. Without the ability to work well together, even when the objective skills look promising, it will be very hard to succeed.

The Recruiting Process

So you decided that it's necessary, you defined the job description and the fundraiser's required traits, and you even earmarked a budget. Now, how do you proceed to recruit, coordinate expectations, sign the contract, hire the new employee, and get to work?

There are two main options for recruiting a fundraising professional. Assuming that the organization doesn't already have someone who can switch hats and become the fundraiser, you can choose to either independently recruit a new employee or use a headhunter.

Independent recruiting. This involves advertising the job description and required traits, receiving applications from candidates, performing a selection process, and choosing the best person. Advertisements should be published in a variety of places: newspapers (regional and national), job search websites and websites dedicated specifically to NGO placement, and professional social media sites (LinkedIn is currently the leading website for this purpose). In addition, try to distribute the advertisement to as many of your contacts as possible so that they will forward it to their own networks, raising the chance that the right person will see it and submit an application. Independent recruitment takes time and resources (depending on the extent and type of advertising), and it is vital to have people who are very familiar with fundraising on the selection team. The final decision must come from the person overseeing fundraising efforts, but to ensure a wise decision, it helps to consult with other professionals.

Recruiting using a headhunter. This is easier in terms of the time investment that the management must make, but also more expensive, because the recruiting company needs to earn a profit too. When using an employment company, be sure to use an appropriate company that is familiar with the field. Over the years, I have received inquiries from headhunters who were looking for fundraisers but had a hard time defining the position and the necessary skills. It sometimes seemed to me that they weren't familiar with the fundraising world. At the final stage of the selection process, the management of the organization should still consult with professionals who can ask the right questions and separate the fairytales from the real deal.

During the recruitment process, two important points should be kept in mind: One is that there aren't that many excellent fundraising professionals; people who are actively involved in the field (and headhunters recruiting in it) will testify to this. The field of professional fundraising is a growing, developing field, and as such, its training system is slowly taking shape, but the demand is still greater than the existing supply. It's not easy to find a professional who is a great fit for your organization. If you've already found one and she's proven herself, make sure to keep her!

Two, the search must be proportionate to the size of the organization, its fundraising objectives, and its financial means. It's hard to convince someone who managed a large hospital's fundraising operation and is accustomed to being paid a high salary to come fundraise for a small organization for much lower pay. If he's interested, he might have a unique altruistic motive, but exercise caution nonetheless.

PROPER COMPENSATION FOR FUNDRAISING PROFESSIONALS

Before the search for candidates for a fundraising position begins, some thought and planning should be dedicated to the issue of compensation. Fundraising is very similar to sales. It's easy to evaluate success or failure, since the focus is on the bottom line: How much did you sell/raise this year? How does that figure compare with your achievements last year? Another similarity between sales and fundraising is the professional's monetary value to the organization. An excellent salesperson and an excellent fundraiser are worth their weight in gold.

What's Important to Fundraisers?

Before we get into dollars and cents, consider what motivates the fundraiser. What drives him to dedicate all of his skills to the cause? What causes him to jump up in the morning, ready to take on the world? What gives him motivation and propels him forward? In short, what's important to fundraisers?

While no two people are the same, there are a few central elements that motivate fundraisers.

Recognition. Fundraising is replete with disappointments. Lots of negative answers. Lots of expectations (of donations) that don't come to fruition. If you get two positive answers for every ten requests you make, you're a lucky person. A fundraiser, whether she admits it or not, needs positive reinforcement from colleagues and superiors. A kind word, encouragement, recognition of achievements when made, a phone call at just the right time to recognize the fundraiser's professionalism, skills, achievements, position, and importance in the organization. At Tel Hai College, I enjoyed working with my CEO Eitan Gedalizon, who was constantly spreading positive energy around him. In the end, we became good friends too. Almost every day of work began with a chat on the phone. He would update me and consult with me, even in areas that weren't related to my responsibilities. Whenever I left the house to go to the airport on Saturday night, he would call to energize me. When I landed back at home, I would call him to report, sharing both the successes and the failures. The energy and reinforcement I received from Eitan was an important part of my professional success during that period.

Integrating into the organization. Naturally, most of a fundraiser's time, attention, and energy is directed outward, toward potential and existing donors. At the same time, however, it is vital for a fundraiser to also be involved in the organization itself, so that its employees (who can and need to help with connections, ideas, and reporting) know him and consider him "one of them." When I was asked once if I preferred to work from home (not due to the need for social distancing for health reasons, as many of us had to do during the 2020 COVID-19 pandemic) or at the organization's offices, I didn't hesitate for a moment. Despite the fact that working from home seems more comfortable, I recognized the importance of being physically present at the organization, getting to know the different people and departments, and being an organic member. In the right context, the organization gives its fundraiser the strength and energy needed for the daily struggle to raise money.

Professional development. Like other professionals in the information industries, fundraisers also need constant learning and enrichment. Participating in professional conferences, events run by other organizations, meetings with colleagues, seminars, and continuing education are all part of this enrichment.

Monetary incentives. A monetary incentive is obviously an important factor that motivates fundraisers. Bonuses are a great way to reward excellent work, especially when funds that exceed the original goal are obtained. Sometimes, a nice monetary bonus or a gift certificate, plus words of appreciation, can also be an energizing and satisfying form of compensation.

That special important ingredient. Every person, and every professional, has individual interests, needs, emotions, and dreams. A manager should try to understand what interests the fundraiser. One of my own interests was teaching karate. When I managed to combine my demanding work, which required frequent travel and even flights overseas, with my passion of running a karate club twice a week, I felt satisfied and content. To do so, however, I had to leave early twice a week to get to the club on time (and this arrangement was even specified in my employment agreement). One workplace accepted this with ease and understanding, since my fundraising results were excellent and there was no question that I worked more than the required hours. At another organization, it was more difficult, despite the fact that my fundraising stats were very good there too. The difference between the approaches of the two organizations regarding combining my karate instruction work with my fundraising work had a significant impact on the way I felt at each place.

Period of the Contract

Fundraising is a process for which it takes time to establish a strong foundation. It's no coincidence that it is often referred to as "development." A candidate who promises to bring in many donations within a short period of time should arouse your suspicion. Especially when an organization does not yet have an existing fundraising infrastructure, management must grant the time to lay a strong foundation. It's a good idea to sign the first employment agreement with your new fundraiser for a period of two years, during which milestones and evaluation points are specified (for example, performing an assessment of the status and pace of advancement every six months). This preliminary period is beneficial for both employer and employee. The employee feels she has time to build the system without feeling exaggerated pressure (although pressure, sometimes a lot of it, will always exist). This kind of arrangement also frees the employer from pressure to improve the employment terms in the event that large successes happen earlier than expected.

Toward the end of the first two years of employment, it's a good idea to analyze the situation and perform an evaluation together, comparing the results with the goals. Assuming that the results achieved are at least satisfactory, from this point onward, the agreement can be extended every year, or a two-year contract can be repeated.

In any event, with a personal agreement, conditions for termination can be set forth based on prior notice, as agreed between the parties. Even with a two-year contract, if the conclusion is reached before the agreement ends that it's just not compatible, the organization will have the option of terminating the fundraiser's employment.

Evaluating Success

How is a fundraising system evaluated? Of course, the bottom line is always the first thing that comes to mind: How much money did the organization receive from donations? But the bottom line isn't everything. Here are a few suggestions of quantitative criteria for annual evaluation of the success of a fundraising system that are especially relevant for systems that are under construction.

Quantitative Criteria for Annual Evaluation

- What is the total amount of donations received?
- How many donors does the organization have?
- How many commitments of future donations were received?
- How many new donors joined the organization's circle of donors?
- How many longtime donors are continuing to donate, and which of these have increased their donations?
- How many donation requests were sent?

- How many meetings to request donations were held with donors?
- How many potential donors visited the organization?
- How many new foundations were engaged?
- How many new partnerships were established?
- Were you able to open up any new markets?
- Were you able to launch any new projects?

Qualitative Criteria for Annual Evaluation

- Scope and level of the organization's marketing materials (website, social media presence, project brochures, and image materials)
- Establishment and operation of an information system to manage donations (DRM)
- Scope of involvement of volunteer leadership

A consistent, ongoing professional process for evaluating a fundraising system's success is important both for the fundraiser and for the management. Time and thought should be invested in determining the criteria, setting evaluation dates, and assessing results. Periodic assessment helps both employee and supervisor step back from their intensive routines and examine their outputs and achievements, as well as failures.

Common Mistakes

Most directors of nonprofits are equipped with a basic understanding of the central areas of activity of their senior employees: finance, human resources, administration, etc. But they often lack experience and understanding when it comes to fundraising. They've simply never dealt with it before. Their challenge is admitting it. I've heard the following statement several times from supervisors: "I really don't know a thing about fundraising, but…" That "but" is usually the problem. What it really means is: I don't understand, but I *think* that I do… With that in mind, what are the classic mistakes that are made when hiring and managing fundraising professionals?

Unrealistic expectations. This happens when the management expects to see their financial graph changing from red to green too soon, with expenses being dwarfed by income. In their minds, just a few phone calls will bring in those wonderful donations, and they expect donation amounts to be high right off the bat.

Isolating the fundraiser. At one of the large organizations that I fundraised for, I encountered the following statement during the first few weeks on the job: "Your success is our success." It took me a while before I realized that this blessing was actually a curse in disguise. It expressed the expectation that I (the fundraiser) would be the one solely responsible for bringing in donations, while he (the well-wisher) looked on from the sidelines without getting his hands dirty doing fundraising work. Good fundraising involves as many of the organization's members as possible, on all levels. Employees, volunteers, volunteer leaders, service recipients, and more. The more people at an organization with fundraising on their agendas, the better.

Failure to inspire identification. The management must not relate to the fundraising professional as a contractor, an external entity whose job is to bring in money. A fundraiser who identifies with the organization, feels excited about the goal and the achievements, and has a strong relationship with its members and those who receive its services will be much more successful when representing and "selling" it.

A Personal Reflection

At the end of the day, a fundraiser's performance is measured by the bottom line: money. How much did you bring in? This job is quantifiable. You can be a nice guy, a hard worker, an engaging speaker, and ask for donations from people all around the world, but in the final analysis, if you don't manage to bring in donations to the organization you represent, you haven't succeeded in your mission. In many ways, a fundraiser is like a salesperson. Both are valued by the numbers – how much they sold or how much they brought into the organization.

But there's a major difference between the salesperson in a business and the fundraiser in a nonprofit organization, and that is the purpose of the money raised. The organization's goal. What the money enables. The satisfaction found in doing good. The joy of making the world a better place, in Hebrew we call this *tikkun olam* (literally, "repair of the world").

Resource development officers must remember and preferably find satisfaction in the fact that they are contributing to the improvement of society on a daily basis, with every step they take. Success in obtaining donations means much more than improving the organization's balance sheet. It makes the world, the state, society, and the community in which we live a better, stronger, healthier place.

Every year before Yom Kippur, the Jewish Day of Atonement when Jews traditionally take stock of their spiritual state (I know many people who also do this before January 1), I mindfully perform a mental review of what positive projects and activities I helped push forward over the past year. For example, how many needy students received a scholarship thanks to donations I solicited? What programs for advancing needy populations did I obtain funding for? On this holiest of days, I also call to mind the Sisyphean labor involved in fundraising, which can sometimes feel terribly frustrating and discouraging. As I stand in prayer, trying to fully be in the here and now, I pray that my efforts and the generosity of the donors I was fortunate to build relationships with will help me, my dear ones, my people, and the whole world to be written in the Book of Life.

CHAPTER 11

FUNDRAISING DURING CRISIS

It's important to keep a healthy balance between seeing reality as it is, even when it isn't encouraging, and maintaining a level of enthusiasm, energy, and optimism.

In early February 2020, I attended the annual Harvard Alumni Association Leadership Conference in Cambridge, Massachusetts. By that point, the world was already awakening to the threat of the coronavirus, which first broke out in China in late 2019. At airports, you could already see people wearing face masks that would have seemed less out of place in an operating room. A feeling of apprehension about physical distancing was in the air. Anyone who coughed or sneezed would draw unwanted stares. Still, the general feeling in early February 2020 was that COVID-19 was a Chinese problem.

Ahead of the conference, the university distributed participant guidelines encouraging personal hygiene and social distancing in order to avoid infection with the mysterious virus. Even skeptics found these directives hard to ignore. Once there, I took a few leisure hours to stroll around Harvard Square, savoring the unique atmosphere of the oldest university in the United States, sampling the famous ice creams – the taste of which hadn't changed since my student days in the '90s – and peeking into the shops surrounding the campus. Everything still seemed calm and tranquil.

Near the end of the conference, on the eve of my return flight to Israel on Turkish Airlines through Istanbul, my wife begged me to wear a protective mask. I wasn't crazy about the idea, but since she asked, I did, only casually removing it for refreshments.

Several weeks later, in early March, a Christian pro-Israel group in the Philippines was to host me as part of a mission integrating fundraising with educational and public relations activities on Israel. By then, COVID-19 had gone from a Chinese virus to a worldwide pandemic. Business and vacation travelers were postponing their trips, and airlines were canceling international flights – especially to the Far East. When I called my Philippine hosts to ask for their assessment, they dismissed my concerns: "We're an island; the coronavirus won't come here." I decided not to let the virus change my plans, but then, three days prior to the long flight, I was forced to cancel it for family reasons. Ten days passed. The coronavirus spread across the globe, with new hotspots emerging in Italy, Spain, the UK, the United States, and elsewhere. Even the Philippines went into a nationwide lockdown.

And so, by mid-March 2020, the grim realization had sunk in that the entire world was dealing with an unprecedented modern-day pandemic. One that threatened not only the lives of millions across the world, but also – and some would say principally – the world economy and the livelihoods of hundreds of millions.

After banning all inbound and outbound flights and shutting down public transportation as the obvious immediate precautions, governments put their citizens into lockdown to cut off the chain of transmission. Whole industries started laying off workers while the workload for essential workers became strenuous and dangerous. Schools and business closed, and people started hoarding food and essential items, while cutting expenses in apprehension of a bad recession. The financial markets crashed. The number of worldwide COVID-19 cases rose steadily, and with them the number of deaths.

By now it was clear that this crisis was like no other, and would have very far-reaching effects on philanthropy. Unlike other recent crises, this one had no geographical boundaries and no projected duration. We would soon discover that there was no telling when the coronavirus would blow over, or what the world in general – and the world of fundraising in particular – would look like in its aftermath. Only one thing was clear: we were facing a world dramatically different from the one we had known at the end of 2019.

During this period, I was managing the fundraising operations of the Max Stern Yezreel Valley College. Overall, on the eve of the coronavirus crisis, the college's fundraising status was relatively good – mainly because we had multiyear commitments for substantial contributions which softened the impact of the crisis, at least in the short term.

My concern was not only for the college, but for its friends and donors, and so our fundraising operation was guided by two principles:

1. **Keep in touch.** The first principle was to maintain a close and compassionate relationship with all our donors and partners, out of an awareness that the crisis compromises us all. In the not so distant past, in an Israeli security crisis, we would be raising money from people who weren't affected, elsewhere in the world, for those living in Israel. The current situation was different. Almost no one had escaped the effects of the coronavirus. The wealthy had also faced the health threat, separation from their loved ones as a result of quarantine and social distancing, heavy financial losses as a result of the economic crash, and an erosion of their sense of personal security. It was essential to internalize this and build up an appropriate plan of action, out of a realization that we had all taken a hit from this and that we all needed some empathy, positive energy, and words of inspiration and hope.

2. **Hold back the ask.** The second principle was not to ask for donations at this stage. In this first, critical stage, it was understood that all available resources should be directed toward needs imposed by the crisis. And our college – which, like most higher education institutions in Israel, had switched to long-distance learning – had practically no impending major expenses created by the coronavirus situation.

The second principle demanded considerable self-discipline. In times of crisis, fundraisers shift into full gear, both in order to make the most of the extreme situation and to channel the restless energy brought about by the crisis into productive action. Early Israeli media coverage of the crisis likened the fight against the virus to a war, which reminded me of the Second Lebanon War in 2006. Tel Hai College tripled the scope of its fundraising during the war and for months following the missiles that rained down on northern Israel. But from my many conversations with donors, board chairs, and others, it was obvious that the focus should be on those directly affected. Exaggeration of nonessential needs in the short term was not only inappropriate, it would also harm the relationship with donors in the long term.

In my work as a fundraiser and consultant, I found myself providing guidance and advice to nonprofit organizations that were grappling with the dilemma of what to do next – and even more crucially, what not to do. We were all in a mindful holding pattern, wanting our next step to be the right step.

And so, over the spring and summer of 2020, I took part in dozens of phone and Zoom conversations with CEOs of philanthropic foundations, fundraisers, donors, and other professionals across the world about the takeaways of the coronavirus crisis. These were the four key questions I asked them:

1. How has fundraising changed in the wake of the ongoing coronavirus crisis?
2. What should organizations and fundraisers do – "Dos"?
3. What should organizations and fundraisers not do – "Don'ts"?
4. What new fundraising trends do you see?

This chapter was written while the story of the COVID-19 crisis was still unfolding, evolving in ways we've never before experienced. But even while the end of this particular crisis is still shrouded in mist, we can be guided by the wisdom and experience of many others to share some inherently valuable lessons and conclusions.

IDENTIFYING AND PREPARING FOR CRISES

Every few years, we're hit with a major crisis of one kind or another. In Israel, crises tend to revolve around security – in the form of war, a military operation, or terror attacks. Elsewhere in the world, crises have come in a variety of different shapes: economic crunches (e.g., the stock market crash of 2008), security situations with an economic aspect (e.g., 9/11 in 2001), or natural disasters (e.g., earthquakes and tsunamis).

When a crisis looms, here are some suggested courses of action.

Identify the crisis. It's human nature to try to push off bad news and to take the view that things will continue as they've always been. It isn't easy or pleasant to recognize that life is drastically changing and that a crisis is unfolding.

But there's no choice. When you're faced with a crisis that's changing the rules of the game and requires specific preparation for an appropriate response, recognize it. Don't turn your back on reality; look it straight in the eye.

Define the crisis. Ask yourself the following questions. Is it a short-term or a long-term affair? Who will be the primary casualties? Will the damage be mainly physical, psychological, or financial – or all three? How will the crisis affect me personally? How will it affect my organization? How will it affect my line of work and my target audience? How will it affect my donors?

Prepare a plan of action. Envision several different scenarios for getting through the crisis. Your scenarios should take into account various ways the crisis might develop, as well as its duration. Similarly, factor in different fundraising scenarios. A striking feature of a major crisis is that it is difficult to prepare a battle plan or a budget for a situation you've never been in. It is therefore desirable to prepare options for a number of scenarios (for example, optimistic, realistic, pessimistic) and to update them frequently.

Revise your plans. Update your projections as the crisis unfolds and its trajectory becomes clearer. One of the most notable features of a major crisis is the characteristic uncertainty. As the situation becomes clearer, the plan of action and the various scenarios have to be adjusted. Daphna, Executive Director of a nonprofit organization dedicated to reducing the digital divide of disadvantaged populations, shares her experience dealing with the COVID-19 crisis: "As soon as we understood that we were in an unprecedented crisis, we began by constructing three reference scenarios, which took into account different levels of possible revenue from government ministries and donations as well as different levels of activity. Every two days we reviewed our revenue flow and the scope of our activity, and made adjustments accordingly. At the same time, we made sure to always have reserves, to give ourselves a financial safety net of at least six months' activity going forward."

Identify and seize opportunities. It's a truism that every crisis opens the door to opportunities as well. During the first few months of the COVID-19 crisis, for instance, Israeli hospitals raked in record donations, many of them completely unsolicited. Philanthropic foundations, companies, and private individuals stepped up because the urgent need was clear. It was the same for charities that supply food for vulnerable populations, as well as for emergency response organizations. At a time when thousands of organizations were crippled in the wake of the health and ensuing economic crisis, there were also nonprofits whose leadership saw an opportunity, initiated an ambitious plan of action, and carried it out. Organizations like that not only did not suffer during the crisis, they even grew.

Strengthen your partners. "Two are better than one," wrote the prophet in Ecclesiastes. Sometimes three and four are even better. In times of crisis, there's a special importance to cooperation and mutual assistance between organizations. Even merger might be an advantage. One of the first insights that came up from an analysis of COVID-19's effects on social service organizations was the need for sincere cooperation between organizations that work in the same field or even in the same community. In ordinary, prosperous times, we can afford to have dozens of organizations engaged in assisting at-risk youth, for example, but in a situation where there's been a drastic fall in overall donations, it's only logical to consider cooperation and even merger between two or more organizations, to eliminate overhead and duplication. This will be appreciated by donors too.

Strengthen and take care of yourself and your team. Even – if not especially – in times of crisis, it's essential to take care of yourself and your team members so everyone will have the motivation, stamina, and ability to cope with long-term challenges. This means personal care, healthy and satisfying food, quality time with spouse and family, adequate amounts of sleep, spiritual growth, fitness, and de-stressing (letting go of stress and tensions). Especially during a crisis, when old habits, organizations, and people are falling apart before your eyes, it's vital to set aside time, attention, and resources for your well-being.

IN A GLOBAL CRISIS, WHAT WILL DONORS DO?
As the coronavirus was spreading around the world in 2020, with the skies almost completely closed to air travel and people hunkered down in their homes in fear of infection and of the economic and social implications of the

worldwide pandemic, it was clear to everyone that fundraising as we knew it would undergo a serious shakeup. At this juncture, I identified an acute need for direct dialogue between philanthropists and the leadership and fundraisers of nonprofit organizations. Everyone was overwhelmed by the situation and uncertain about how they could continue making the world a better place. Ultimately there was one question on every fundraiser's mind: What will the donors do? How will the crisis affect their ability and willingness to donate? Every organization that depends on fundraising would be influenced by the answers to these questions, but there was no shared platform or venue for asking the donors directly for their thoughts and plans.

I love bringing people together, so I teamed up with my friend Maya Lapid Edut, director of the Israeli initiative Committed to Give, to arrange a series of online meetings between prominent donors from Israel and across the world, directors, fundraisers, board members of nonprofit organizations, and others. Burning philanthropic issues were discussed while donors fielded questions such as the following:

- How have the health and economic crises affected your giving priorities?
- What advice would you give to organizations that are trying to raise money during this period?
- What types of updates would you like to receive from organizations you support, and how often?
- What are your criteria for making donations during this period? Are they different from the criteria you used in the past?
- Has the responsibility of lay leadership changed during the crisis? How?

One of the most intriguing issues that surfaced during these discussions was the tension between two important and time-honored Jewish principles: on the one hand, "Charity begins at home," and on the other, "All Israel is responsible for one another." As is well known, Israeli organizations have received substantial contributions from Jewish (and non-Jewish) donors worldwide, since long before the founding of the state. Most of these donors have also been contributing to causes and organizations close to their hearts in their home cities and countries. The economic crisis of 2020 and the distress of communities across the world put the continued viability of this funding from abroad in serious question. It was unclear, for instance, that a Canadian philanthropist who needed to support his struggling local synagogue, Jewish day school, and Jewish summer camp would feel the need to donate to an organization in Israel.

For this reason, we asked some of the Jewish donors in the Diaspora: How has the coronavirus, which has hit almost every country and community in the world, affected your willingness and ability to donate to organizations in Israel?

Granted that the donors who participated in these conversations were far above average in terms of their commitment to Zionism and supporting Israeli organizations, but it was nevertheless profoundly encouraging and moving to hear that their deep and steadfast commitment to Israel was undiminished. At the same time, it was evident that with the fortunes of many of these donors considerably smaller than they had been at the outbreak of the virus, and with urgent needs back home up dramatically, many Israeli organizations would see a decrease in donations from abroad.

LESSONS FOR HANDLING CRISES

When we take a look at fundraising during the coronavirus crisis, it's a challenge to isolate and extract lessons and insights likely to prove useful in preparing for future crises.

I recommend recalling the following principles.

Lay Leadership Is Crucial

The lay leadership of an organization must be real, organic partners in its long-term plan. Again and again, I've been told by board members that organizations that gave their donors a sense of belonging and even of ownership over the organization's functioning, resilience, and future were rewarded when their donors not only remained committed to the organization, despite the crisis and its financial and psychological implications, but actually increased their commitments dramatically. Raya, a well-known Israeli venture philanthropist, emotionally described why she had invested her heart and soul in lobbying the government on behalf of one of "her" organizations, when budgetary cuts threatened to significantly reduce its funding.

To sum it up in one sentence: long-term investment in recruiting, cultivating, empowering, and embracing lay leadership is essential not only for an organization's smooth functioning and financial resilience in ordinary times, but also for its preparedness for crises.

Populations Must Be Served with Empathy

One characteristic of the coronavirus crisis of 2020 was the fact that it affected everyone, hitting every strata of society almost everywhere in the world. Obviously, a homeless person in San Francisco may have been hit worse than a wealthy one from Palo Alto. But the wealthy person was almost certainly affected as well: in terms of health; confidence in his or her financial resilience; inability to leave the house, travel, or meet people; in terms of general uncertainty; and so on.

Thus, when fundraisers and leaders of organizations were called upon to do their jobs during the COVID-19 crisis, they had to operate within four circles of empathy and attentiveness, which overlap and tie into one another:

1. **Empathy for the populations they serve.** Program participants almost certainly suffered: disabled populations; students; the sick; elderly people in nursing homes; members of cultural, educational, and artistic institutions; and so on.
2. **Empathy for their employees.** Workers in social service organizations, especially those that rely on donations, have been especially hard hit in the coronavirus crisis. Many were fired, sent on unpaid leave, saw their salaries cut, or endured deteriorating work conditions. Many of those who worked in nonprofits aimed at helping disadvantaged members of society found themselves joining the ranks of the casualties overnight. In addition to the challenge of keeping their organizations afloat and maintained, organization leaders had to take care of the morale and livelihoods of their staffs.
3. **Empathy for themselves.** A fundraiser who doesn't succeed in maintaining a basic level of health, energy, and optimism won't be able to properly fulfil the fundraising role. This is true even in normal times, and much more so during a crisis.
4. **Empathy for donors.** In ordinary times, it's essential to remember that donors are after all human beings with their own strengths and weaknesses, hopes and fears, just like the rest of us. In times of crisis, it's

just as important to remember that they too are vulnerable, in need of empathy, encouragement, positive energy, a listening ear, and caring. If you call your donor and focus only on what you want, without pausing to ask yourself what you can give, you'll miss an opportunity to do the right thing.

An Organization Must Have a Clear Mission

In order to raise funds, managers must define, clarify, and explain the essence and unique mission of their organizations. This is always the case, but even more so during a crisis, when emergency needs increase dramatically overnight; competition over vital resources intensifies; and the energy, attention span, and patience of donors decreases. Many donors told me that in a time of crisis especially, they expect to understand precisely and quickly what is wanted from them, who and what it's needed for, and what, precisely, will be done with the money they're being asked to donate.

Realism Must Be Balanced with Optimism

It's important to keep a healthy balance between seeing reality as it is, even when it isn't encouraging, and maintaining a level of enthusiasm, energy, and optimism.

Ron Schiller, author of best-selling books on fundraising and partner in the Aspen Leadership Group, describes the Chief Development Officer (CDO) as a Chief Confidence Officer (CCO), or Chief Optimism Officer (COO). In times of crisis, the organization's team as well as the lay leadership is liable to sink into pessimism and despair. Along with thoughtful vision and a realistic and considered plan of action, the role of the Chief Development Officer is to raise the organization's confidence and optimism in its abilities in general, and its fundraising abilities in particular. Thus, the question that needs to be asked is not "Will we succeed in raising funds?" but "How will we succeed in raising funds?"

Just like any political, social, or financial leader, anyone involved in fundraising must have the ability to deal with the here and now, with the immediate and urgent, while at the same time looking forward over the horizon, remembering, knowing, and communicating the recognition that after the great darkness will come light.

TO ASK OR NOT TO ASK

In a time of crisis, it's important to develop a sane and balanced approach to the dilemma of whether or not to request a donation. I've already alluded to this dilemma, but it's important enough to emphasize again. CEOs and fundraisers always need to raise money. This need only intensifies in times of crisis. But despite the pressure and the temptation to use crises as leverage to secure more funds, and despite the concern that funding might suffer as a result of the crisis, the management of an organization needs to read the map correctly and act accordingly.

When to Refrain from Requesting Donations

In times of crisis, especially when the financial pressure is up, the management turns up the heat. When you see others raising money and recounting their successes, the pressure to ask for a donation grows even more powerful. Despite the pressure, sometimes it's necessary to have restraint. An insensitive solicitation to a donor whose business or investments have been hit financially could give offense and even damage the relationship with you and with your organization.

Almost everyone has been hit by the coronavirus. There are a few who profited from the crisis, or will from its aftermath, but in general, the trend is significant financial losses.

- **Capital losses.** A donor who earned a 10 percent yield on capital before the crisis and saw a 30 percent loss at the peak of the crisis will feel less capable of contributing.
- **Dramatic decline in revenue.** Donors who were able to give generously due to their profits in industries that ground to a halt almost overnight during the crisis will be forced to drastically cut or limit the scope of their donations. Notable examples of this in the coronavirus crisis are the travel, auto, and oil industries.

When I spoke with Scott, chair of a large philanthropic foundation, I asked him: "Would donors who suffered drastic losses stop donating entirely? Or are there circumstances under which they would continue donating despite everything?" After pondering a minute, Scott replied that two conditions have to be met for such a donor to continue donating: one, that the organization soliciting the donation really is close to the donor's heart, and not just another name on the usual list of charities. And two, that the organization seeking the donation really does need it, and may be unable to survive or fulfill its mission without it.

If neither of these two conditions are met, it's a mistake – even a chutzpah – to solicit funding from a donor whose finances have suffered during the crisis. And how are you supposed to know whether the donor has been affected? This question brings us back to an earlier principle: keep in touch with your donors. Listen to them. Empathize with them. In the process, you'll also learn how they're doing and how they and their associates have been affected by the crisis.

Another thing to watch out for is opportunistic fundraising: requests for donations that seek to exploit the atmosphere of the crisis for purposes not linked to the urgent response to the crisis. Donors expressed to me that this doesn't just upset them, it makes them less likely to donate to an organization in the future, even when their finances improve.

It's very important not to burn bridges with donors during a crisis out of recklessness and insensitivity. A relationship that took years to build up can be destroyed in a single day. While it is always important to identify when it's a good time to request a donation and when it isn't, during a crisis the importance of this is magnified.

When You Should Request a Donation

Organizations directly engaged in the response to the crisis (e.g., in the COVID-19 crisis, hospitals, medical organizations, food organizations) can and should solicit donations during the crisis. However, now more than ever it is important to make the request focused. Don't make a general request for assistance, but a focused, clear, human, and authentic request. If you feel any uncertainty about whether a request for aid would be appropriate or not, it's recommended to take a "soft" approach. For instance, instead of bluntly asking, "Could you donate such and such a sum…," you can choose an approach that takes account of the donor's willingness to hear about the cause and your needs, while also listening carefully to the impact of the crisis on his or her ability to donate. This gentle approach might find expression in a sentence such as this: "The crisis has significantly increased the demand for services that we offer to the public… Over the next few months, we're going to need $XX to meet the needs of ZZ people. Do you know of any people or foundations that would be interested in being part of meeting this need or finding a solution?"

Alan Gill provides an answer to the question of whether to request a donation when he touches on the human search for meaning: "In times of crisis, people are more than ever looking to find meaning in their lives and existences. People want to be part of something useful and productive. The reaction of those who want to help moves along a spectrum from 'joining something positive' to 'being a savior.' No one wants to end up in a situation where years down the line, when they're asked how they used their resources, abilities, and connections to help during the coronavirus crisis of 2020, they'll be left without an answer."

As for the organizations themselves, they can't allow themselves to hold back from soliciting a donation, if it really is necessary. After all, they don't just represent themselves, but everyone who makes use of their services. It's incumbent on them to candidly represent their real need for a donation in a time of crisis – even if they realize that many won't donate – out of a firm knowledge that some people will be interested in donating.

Scott expands on this subject: "You should understand and empathize with the donors' troubles, but you don't need to identify with them too much. Your job is to secure funding to continue your holy work." This is always true, and even more so in a time of crisis. For example, Scott told me, at the peak of the coronavirus, he called several institutions in his city in the United States that were on the front line of dealing with the ramifications of the coronavirus. The philanthropic foundation he runs donated $1 million to one food bank, without the money even being solicited.

MINDFUL FUNDRAISING IN TIMES OF CRISIS

The Buddhist principle of *anicca* (impermanence) applies to fundraising during crises. According to this principle, one of the three marks of existence in Buddhism, everything in life is impermanent and changing. A flower blooms, withers, and falls. Clouds give way to sunlight. Nothing remains constant and in the same state forever. A favorite Buddhist proverb says, in this spirit: "It's impossible to bathe twice in the same river."

The principle of *anicca* can help us in overcoming the challenges of life. Pain that troubles us today will disappear tomorrow. Oppressive weather conditions will clear up. And the same goes for fundraising during crisis. When the COVID-19 crisis broke out in early 2020, many veteran CEOs and fundraisers looked back to the worldwide economic crisis of 2008 to try to derive a few useful lessons for the present. At the end of 2008, we saw a financial and economic collapse that wiped out entire fortunes and – among other things to be laid at the racketeer Bernie Madoff's door – crushed many donors and philanthropic foundations. But the world recovered from the crisis, and the second decade of the twenty-first century witnessed a period of unprecedented economic growth and a sharp rise in levels of charitable donations. Had the leaders of social service organizations in 2008 been endowed with prophetic vision that allowed them to foresee the rapid recovery of the economy and philanthropy, that would doubtless have been a stabilizing and calming influence. In the absence of prophecy, it's worthwhile to make use of the *anicca* principle, to internalize the transience of life and the transience of crises.

In the Book of Genesis, as a finale to the drama of the Flood in which the righteous Noah and his family are saved from a deluge that wipes out almost the entire human race, the covenant of the rainbow in the clouds between God and humanity is described: "And God said: 'This is the token of the covenant which I make between Me and you and every living creature that is with you, for perpetual generations: I have set My bow in the cloud, and it shall be for a token of a covenant between Me and the earth.… And the bow shall be in the cloud; and I will look upon it, that I may remember the everlasting covenant between God and every living creature of all flesh that is upon the earth'" (Genesis 9:12–13, 16).

If we are to distill and point to one essential lesson for fundraising during crises, when we need to keep up our holy work in a world that's changing, tottering, and sometimes chaotic, it is an integration of teachings and traditions spanning thousands of years, from Buddha and Noah to the coronavirus in our own times: *think lucidly, see reality as it is, remember that nothing stays the same, maintain optimism and hope, be human, and always hold on to faith.*

CHAPTER 12

THE TEN COMMANDMENTS OF RESOURCE DEVELOPMENT

Thou shalt invest in thine resource development operation!

Now to put everything we've discussed into practice. Here are my ten rules for building or upgrading a resource development operation.

The Ten Commandments of Resource Development	
I. Decide the time has come	VI. List giving opportunities
II. Identify your uniqueness	VII. Train yourself and your staff
III. Focus your vision	VIII. Build Friends groups
IV. Define your assets	IX. Cultivate donors
V. Create a work plan	X. Use your secret weapon

1. DECIDE THE TIME HAS COME

Almost every director of a nonprofit knows that fundraising has to be done and is even under pressure to do so. But there are always a host of reasons for putting off building a fundraising system: there's no time, there's not enough money, the global economy is in the doldrums, there are no good fundraising staff to be found, no one would give to an organization like ours anyway, other organizations are better than we are, next year, after the holidays.

The most important step in creating an in-house fundraising operation is simply to decide that the time has come to do so. This is the first question I ask at my first consulting session with the leadership of any nonprofit: "Have you decided that the time is right to fundraise, and are you fully committed to your decision?" All too often I get the impression that the organization's leaders aren't sufficiently dedicated to the task; or alternatively, that their decision is being driven by motivations that just aren't strong enough, such as pressure on the CEO from the board of directors, or because everyone else is doing it. These kinds of external motivations signal a lack of real internal commitment to the process.

Sometimes it's better to delay getting involved in fundraising. It demands a considerable investment of time, energy, financial resources, and managerial attention, and it requires drawing on the goodwill of supporters and friends. It's often better not to begin at all than to set off halfheartedly.

2. IDENTIFY YOUR ORGANIZATION'S UNIQUENESS

Competition for the hearts and wallets of funders has always been fierce, but with the increase in numbers of nonprofit organizations and the rapid growth in the number of fundraisers, it's becoming ever more so. In the United States alone, tens of thousands of organizations are competing for funders' attention, sympathy, and concern – and ultimately, for their money. Many of these organizations operate in similar arenas, such as youth at risk, sports, higher education, healthcare, and the environment.

Every CEO, chairperson, or fundraiser must be able to offer convincing answers to the following questions:

- What is it that we do best in this city/country/world?
- What makes us special compared to others who are active in the same field?
- Why should funders give to us and not to another similar organization?

Or to put it most starkly:

- How does our work make the world a better place?
- How would the world suffer if our work were to cease or be curtailed?

It's not enough to say that "we're doing good work" or "we need funding." In order to survive and thrive in the big wide world of fundraising, it's essential to identify and emphasize your organization's uniqueness. Here's an example from Israeli higher education.

In Israel there are a number of institutions whose unique identity is obvious:

- The Hebrew University of Jerusalem is the academic institution of Jerusalem – the holy city, the cradle of the monotheistic religions.
- The Technion–Israel Institute of Technology is Israel's leading technological academic institution, an incubator for training the leaders of Israel's high-tech industry. It's Israel's MIT.
- Ben-Gurion University of the Negev is committed to the social and economic development of Israel's southern periphery.
- Tel Aviv University has an identity that reflects the city of Tel Aviv itself: open, liberal, secular, cosmopolitan, and as much a part of the global village as it is of the Israeli landscape.

But what about Bar-Ilan University and others? These universities (at least at the time of writing) are still searching for their unique identities.

Bar-Ilan University, for example, always had quite a religious image. It was considered an institution with plenty of religiously observant students and a conservative atmosphere, but lacking in academic excellence. The heads of the university have worked hard to try to change this image by investing considerable resources in developing such areas as brain science, nanotechnology, and engineering, sometimes even at the expense of the humanities.

When I arrived at the Max Stern Yezreel Valley College, I learned that one of the main challenges in resource development is identifying the characteristics that make an organization different and unique.

The problem was that we didn't have a particular academic field in which we could claim to be the leading college in Israel. Even the very basic claim that we were engaged in preparing populations in Israel's geographical and socioeconomic periphery for the labor market wasn't strong enough, because most of the degree programs – such as sociology, education, economics, and human services – were in the humanities and the social sciences, not practical employment-focused fields such as engineering.

Without any obvious singular characteristic of the organization as a whole, I decided to define the uniqueness of some of the college's activities. So, for example, I focused on a program in the college's nursing department called "Opportunity for Success," which trained first- and second-generation immigrants from Ethiopia to work as nurses with an academic degree. The program was clear and well structured, served a population that was without doubt in need of support, and became very popular with donors.

The Galilee Center for Studies in Jewish-Christian Relations is an even better example. We decided to create something that hadn't been done before – to reach out to the community of pro-Israel Christians, which numbers about 300 million people worldwide, and to establish a center in Israel that would be the first of its kind. Unlike hundreds of other nonprofits, which seek funding from Israel-supporting Christians solely for their own purposes, we set ourselves the task of understanding these supporters' needs and finding a way to meet them. This process of envisioning and developing a work plan and recruiting an academic director for the program took about a year. But when it was complete, we were able to successfully raise the necessary funds in Europe and the United States and establish the center. Subsequently, the center became a significant lightning rod for attracting funders from around the world to support the organization's other development needs.

An innovative educational organization approached me for help in establishing an in-house resource development operation. At our first consultation meeting, I raised the question of the organization's uniqueness. I asked them questions to help define their focus: "Why would people want to donate to you, rather than to anyone else? What makes your organization special?" At the end of the first meeting, I left them with homework and more questions to help them clarify their purpose and vision.

A few weeks later, I got a call from the parents' representative who was to be involved in setting up the fundraising system. Her background as a marketing director at an international corporation suggested that this would be an easy task for her, but this turned out not to be the case.

"I'm stuck. I've spoken to a number of people who are active in the organization, and they all struggled to answer the question you asked us, about our uniqueness. Most of the answers I got were about what's wrong that we're trying to fix. But we hit a wall. We couldn't find a strong, persuasive positive claim as to why donors should support us as opposed to other organizations."

I answered that if the active members of the organization couldn't think of good reasons to donate to it, they would certainly find it difficult to persuade others to do so. I proposed a structured process that would help her with this and enable her to overcome her frustrations. But in truth, I was not surprised by the fact that no one had a good answer for her. It's not at all unusual. Most of the time, we are entirely caught up in our everyday routines and daily struggles, and it seems obvious to us that what we do is important and meaningful. But when someone asks us to define this importance, to explain the worth of our work and persuade others of it, we have nothing to say in response.

3. FOCUS YOUR ORGANIZATION'S VISION

I often come across directors of organizations who are looking to raise funds but struggle to answer what seems like a simple, trivial question. What is your organization's vision? What is its importance for the world, for the country, for the community, for individuals? How do you picture the world in a few years' time, after your organization's work has made it a better place?

I recommend using a series of guiding questions to help define your organizational vision. For example: How will the world (or the individual, community, society, the region, the city, etc.) be improved by your organization's activities? Or conversely: How would the world look different if your organization ceased to exist? If the answer to the first question is "I'm not sure," and the answer to the second question is "Just the same," then you need to give some serious thought to your organization's importance and uniqueness, because it will raise red flags about your legitimacy in raising funds from donors.

The world of fundraising is competitive and cruel. You compete with tens, hundreds, or even thousands of other organizations over every donor and every donation. They, too, are trying to make the world a better place. They, too, are trying to get donors to buy into their dream and their goals. Fundraisers must be able to articulate and present a clear and confident message about why their organization in particular is worthy of the donor's support.

4. DEFINE YOUR ASSETS

People often ask me: "What's most important to highlight in our fundraising work: Our difficulties, problems, and deficiencies? Or our strengths, advantages, and assets?"

I've always been a big proponent of asset-based fundraising. It's not only more enjoyable, it's more appropriate and more respectful. (I'm grateful to my friend and mentor the late Professor Art Naparstek from Cleveland, from whom I learned this approach.) Moreover, people are attracted to success. Donors are reluctant to give to an organization that's on the verge of collapse – to an institution with run-down buildings and lawns overrun with weeds, whose future seems uncertain.

An organization's assets are not necessarily physical. An essential element of fundraising is defining our assets, understanding them, and using them wisely. What, then, are the assets of a nonprofit organization?

Physical Assets

This is what people think of first in terms of an organization's assets. These include the organization's liquid assets, investments, endowment, and any other financial assets along with physical property: buildings, equipment, and so on. As we are about to see, these are not the only assets an organization holds, but they are of course important and must be well managed for the security of the organization.

Human Assets

Staff. All the people employed by the organization have their own talents and connections. Even a student working part-time may have links to potential donors.

It's important to involve the entire staff in fundraising goals and tasks. The fundraiser, with the full backing of the organization's management, must educate the staff to "think fundraising." They need to be enthused, to have a strong sense of the organization's fundraising needs and opportunities. Everyone knows someone. Everyone can call someone. Everyone can be an advocate. The more the organization's staff are committed to the fundraising cause, the better. Incidentally, this is one of the reasons it's best for fundraisers to work from the organization's physical offices as much as possible, rather than from home (unless extraordinary circumstances such as a pandemic make this impossible, in which case technological workarounds should be used to the fullest extent to ensure the highest possible degree of communication among colleagues). Interaction with the other staff is important, not just because of office politics, but also so as to get everyone on board with the fundraising mission and to be in the know about what new programs are going on.

This was how I was able to begin building a broad network of relationships with donors in one of the richest areas of the United States. One day, an American student studying at Tel Hai College came into my office and said that her father was a board member of a philanthropic foundation that supported students. She introduced me to him, and he held an event at which I was able to meet his fellow donors at the foundation. The foundation began supporting our institution, I got to know other donors in the area through these contacts, and the rest is history.

Boards of directors/governors. Boards of directors, governors, or any other form of lay leadership structure should be an important part of the nonprofit organization's fundraising efforts. In most cases, donating and bringing in donors is defined as one of the central responsibilities of lay leaders.

Lay leaders can often be very helpful with links to new donors, opening doors and being advocates for the organization, and granting it greater legitimacy. Without them, to use a military metaphor, fundraisers are just lone soldiers out in the field, with no help and no backup.

No one should expect that lay leaders will willingly volunteer to help with fundraising. Naturally, it's much easier to give advice, to take part in meetings and discussions, and to make decisions about the organization's future than it is to start making calls to potential donors, to ask for favors, open doors, and especially to personally solicit donations to the organization.

As a result, lay leaders have to be motivated to help with fundraising efforts. Fundraisers have to do their homework on their lay leaders, find out who they know, who is in their circle of friends, what boards they sit on, where they live, and so on. Armed with this information, you need to sit down face-to-face with select board members (some can be more helpful than others) and ask them to open their lists of contacts to help out.

I had the pleasure of working with the former Israeli finance minister Avraham "Beiga" Shochat when he was Chairman of the Board of Trustees of Tel Hai College. During the Second Lebanon War in 2006, we asked Avraham to help us raise funds for scholarships to students, due to concerns that the rocket attacks would deter students from attending an institution in the Upper Galilee.

Avraham got to work, calling around to senior figures in the Israeli business community. For several weeks during the war and afterwards, I'd get brief calls from him: "Write this down: Company X, NIS 200,000. Call so-and-so. He promised me he'd give us the money." In two weeks, Avraham raised about a million shekels for student scholarships. But the most important door he opened for me at that time was to the IDB Group, one of Israel's largest conglomerates. As a result of that introduction and what it led to, Tel Hai's eastern campus now boasts the IDB Library. More about this later on.

Existing donors. Existing donors are the best route to new potential donors. Someone who is already financially and emotionally invested is now committed to the organization. They also serve as role models for new donors, who often want to know who has already given to your organization. Moreover, they know the organization and its fundraising needs, and in most cases know you, the fundraiser. In short, there's no one better than an existing donor for helping the organization find and reach new donors. However, not every donor is willing to share contacts and introduce you to others. A longstanding donor from Canada once told me openly: "I'd rather give you more money myself than ask a friend to donate to you. Any friend I ask will immediately ask me to give to an organization he supports in return. This way, it costs me less…"

In short, identify, nurture, and ask for help from donors who are willing to use their contacts and the goodwill of their friends to open doors for you. It's important that you do this with finesse and consideration, without pressuring the donor in any way. Being overly assertive or aggressive is likely to anger or insult the donor, leaving your erstwhile ally resentful toward you and the organization you represent. Any help you get from a donor – money, contacts, opening doors – has to be given freely, wholeheartedly, and happily.

Treat their time with respect and don't waste it. In the words of the Arabic saying: "If your friend is made of honey, don't lick him up entirely."

Past donors. At one of the organizations where I led the fundraising operations, there were two buildings that bore the name of an American donor. When I began reviewing the list of historical donors to the organization, I was told that they had never had a relationship with this donor, because his gift was raised by representatives of the Jewish Federation system in the United

States who had refused (for obvious reasons) to allow the organization to have direct contact with him.

Not deterred, I waited patiently for a few years, and when the veteran fundraiser of the Federation retired, I was able (with her blessing) to make contact with this donor, who by now was about ninety years old. I traveled to meet him at his impressive home on the coast, armed with videos showing the important work being done in the buildings he had donated and with a beautiful framed certificate of recognition. We hit it off immediately. A relationship began, and I came again to visit him a few months later. At the end of the meeting, I left with a pledge of a generous new donation, which put his name on another building.

Never give up on past donors! A donor who has already given once – as long as the experience was a positive one, which we know is not always the case – is very likely to be willing to give again. I call this approach the "dry well strategy." When you look for water, there's a better chance of finding it in a well that once gave water than by digging new wells in uncharted territory.

Businesses. Traditionally, an organization's donor base has three parts: private donors, philanthropic foundations, and businesses. The expectation that private businesses have an obligation to give back to society and the community rather than just making profits for the company's owners or shareholders has been gaining currency for some time. There is almost no serious company today that does not invest some effort and resources into this area. When mapping an organization's assets for fundraising purposes, it's important to make contact with businesses that might support it. This mapping should take into account several criteria:

1. **Location.** A company located in a geographical area connected to a nonprofit's activities might be very interested in donating to it. There are even companies that invest in philanthropy in an area they are planning to enter or in which they are seeking to expand their activities. By giving to a well-known cause that enjoys public consensus, the company can position and brand itself (and its products and services) in a positive way in that area.
2. **Field of activity.** When mapping assets in the business sector, identify which enterprises are active in the same field as you and approach them first. Food

companies will give to organizations working on food security, including donating food to soup kitchens. High-tech companies will give to organizations developing technological youth leadership. Banks will help promote financial education and financial planning among families in poverty. Law firms will support legal clinics and community advocacy. And so on.

3. **Network of contacts.** Though companies usually publish criteria according to which they give donations, ultimately, funding decisions are made by people within the company. Making contact with a senior official who can be an advocate for your organization can garner positive attention and help you secure the company's support.

The story of Michael demonstrates the importance of personal contacts. I have known Michael, a leading business figure in Israel, for many years. Our paths first crossed on a project for Israeli-Arab collaboration in which we were both involved. I invited him to visit my college. It took a few months to set the visit up, and when he arrived, he said, "I don't know why I'm here, but you invited me, so I came." He met with some of the students in various programs, was introduced to the president of the institution, and eventually promised to deliver a lecture telling the fascinating story of the corporation he had led for many years.

At the end of the meeting, I asked him to donate to one of our flagship programs. He didn't commit, but suggested introducing me to one of his friends, another leading businessman, who was philanthropically active in a similar area. "If he doesn't help you," he said, "get back to me." This introduction didn't result in a donation, and I was careful to keep him updated throughout the process. Sometime after that initial visit, he did indeed return and gave his lecture. When it was over, I reminded him about the donation. "On a personal level, I only give to a particular city where I concentrate all my philanthropic efforts, but I'll put you in touch with my corporation's director of community investment."

And he did. I submitted a request for program support to the corporation's community responsibility fund, making sure to let the head of the fund know who referred me to her. Throughout, I was careful to keep Michael updated, and about six months after his initial visit, I heard from the head of the foundation that we had been awarded a grant. If I hadn't been referred by Michael, and if his involvement hadn't been known to those involved in assessing our grant request, I'm not sure we would even have been considered for a major gift. Opening doors and advocacy is critical for fundraising from companies, no less than for fundraising from individuals and philanthropic foundations.

Brand, History, and Reputation Assets

Brand. Just like businesses, nonprofits have brands. The brand has great fundraising value. The American Cancer Association, for example, is the organization that the public most associates with when discussing eliminating cancer, and thus it enjoys full legitimacy to raise funds for its purpose, like the World Wildlife Fund, a venerable, historic organization that was once recognized by its cute giant panda logo. An organization's image, whether in the local community or state or internationally, can be either an asset or a burden for fundraising. It's important to understand the organization's brand, to develop it or repair it if necessary, and to leverage it wherever possible.

Historic achievements. Past achievements can be an asset for fundraising, but they are only useful if they are not undermined by the events of the present. Overreliance on nostalgia and historic accomplishments can make an organization irrelevant.

5. CREATE A WORK PLAN AND SET MILESTONES

It's very easy to lose focus in fundraising work. The fundraising professional, who is sometimes the only person in the organization's resource development department, has to engage in a broad range of activities. In most cases, these include:

- **Meetings.** Meet with existing donors, potential donors, and their representatives; colleagues, managers, and other staff within the organization; friends and acquaintances; and more.
- **Participation in events and conferences.** Conferences provide an excellent opportunity to meet new people, renew and nurture existing relationships, and gather and renew information. Most of the real work at conferences happens outside the lecture halls – in corridors, showrooms, the cafeteria, and on the golf or tennis court.
- **Fundraising trips.** Travel to other regions, states, or countries.

- **Hosting donor and delegation visits.** Research, prepare for, rehearse, and conduct visits from donors and organizational partners.
- **Getting to know the organization.** Look for stories that can be shared and leveraged.
- **Preparing requests to donors.** Collect information, write and edit requests, and submit documents.
- **Reporting to donors.** Prepare appropriate reports and devise new and creative ways of keeping donors updated about how their funds are being used.
- **Preparing marketing and PR materials.** Come up with creative ideas and make sure they are implemented professionally.
- **Maintaining contact with donors.** This can be done by phone, email, Zoom, social networks, and best of all, face-to-face.
- **Creating new donor relationships.** Network, including leveraging the contacts of existing donors.
- **Collecting information.** Know about new and existing donors; stay abreast of competitors, trends, etc.
- **Internal updates.** Consult with and market within the organization vis-à-vis superiors, directors, lay leaders, colleagues, and staff members.
- **Maintaining information systems.** Update donor information details and add new donors.

Because of this huge range of activities, and because a fundraiser's work is never done (however big the organization you work for, there will always be needs that aren't being met and donors you haven't yet reached), it is supremely important to strive to maintain focus – to keep to a well-defined work plan, differentiate between what is important and what isn't, and be able to deal not only with urgent issues but also (and mainly) with the tasks that are truly important.

At one time, I ran a relatively large resource development department at a university. I came in after a fairly traumatic period for the institution and found myself working sixteen-hour days to solve internal problems, put out fires, and resolve crises. After a few months, I realized that I wasn't doing enough on the main job I was hired to do – raise money. I started asking myself every day, normally in the afternoon, the following question: "What have I done today to raise money?" When the answer was "nothing," I would make an effort to do something by the end of the day – make a call to a donor, send a letter, set a meeting to ask for funding, or any other fundraising activity that, if successful, would have the practical result of bringing in money.

6. LIST YOUR NEEDS AND GIVING OPPORTUNITIES

A few weeks before New Year's Eve, I was approached at the gym by Yoram, a young principal of a local high school with a high number of at-risk youth. "I'd like to ask you about some fundraising issues," he said.

"Sure, how can I help you?" I replied.

"Well, a few days ago, I got a call from a successful businessman. He told me: 'I read about your school on the internet, and I was really impressed with how you implement technology; you're doing wonderful work. I'd like to help. What do you need?' Sagi, I didn't know what to tell him. We need so many things. How do you answer a question like that?"

"Yoram," I replied, "this is a classic question. It's one you want to hear and need to be prepared for. You're the principal of the school and the person responsible for fundraising; if I woke you up in the middle of the night and asked what you need, you should be able to immediately respond with a list of needs and giving opportunities. This should be burned into your brain."

Every fundraiser, CEO, chairperson, or any other person engaged in resource development must have a detailed and precise list of giving opportunities for their organization. This kind of document goes by many names: "project proposals," "donation cards," "funding requests," "sponsorship proposals," and so on. The name matters far less than the content. The document must have the answer to the question that every fundraiser wants to hear from potential donors: "What do you need?" or "How can I help?"

7. TRAIN YOURSELF AND YOUR STAFF

Many times, I've heard people say, "I just don't have what it takes. I can't fundraise." Or, in a slightly different version: "He was born with the ability to raise money. He's never had to learn how." There's no question that some people are more talented, more enthusiastic, and more willing to fundraise than others. But as in any other occupation, everyone can learn and improve.

My teacher, the late Professor Roger Fisher, founded the field of negotiation studies at Harvard Law School as a practice that could be learned and studied. Roger would tell us, his students, how he would be challenged repeatedly with the question "Can you really improve your negotiating ability? Isn't it just something you're born with?" His response to these naysayers was always the same: "Even the number one tennis player in the world and the Olympic 100-meter gold medalist constantly train and try to improve themselves." In fundraising, too, there are those who were born with the essential attributes for this work, and there are those who have developed them: interpersonal communication, presenting skills, persuasiveness, broad general knowledge, and so on. But the best can always improve, and even those who find it hard – just as in sports – can learn, get better, and advance.

Ahead of important meetings and presentations, and especially before making an ask, I practice what to say, and how to say it, several times. On occasion I have even recorded myself repeatedly, so that I can critique and improve my own speaking. Before fundraising meetings, I sometimes practice in front of the mirror, not only so as to polish my presentation skills ahead of a specific meeting, but also to get into the mindset of asking for a donation.

A popular cliché has it that the difference between Israeli and American professionals, when it comes to preparing for important meetings, is that Israelis spend 10 percent of their time on preparing for the meeting and 90 percent on the meeting itself, while Americans spend 90 percent of their time on careful preparation and only 10 percent on the meeting. The precise sociological anecdote is less important than the deeper meaning of this idea. Train yourself and your staff. Honing your skills and preparing carefully for meetings, presentations, and discussions improves your chances of being able to persuade people to support your organization. It can even be worth investing in professional help, such as a presentation skills workshop.

8. BUILD FRIENDS GROUPS

These are similar to boards of directors or governors, but are different in that their members have no legal responsibility toward the organization. People join affinity groups as a statement of interest and support, having either attended events or donated in the past or planning to donate in the future, and in the knowledge that their presence will give more legitimacy for others to donate to and identify with the organization. Affinity groups may engage in organizing events, fundraising drives, activities to increase the organization's public profile, recruiting new supporters, and more. Members of the organization's affinity groups, if there are any, can be an important asset for the fundraiser. Make them feel valued and cherished, and use their help wisely.

Any fundraiser who expects to succeed on the basis of his or her work alone is doomed to failure. A single person trying to go it alone – even if blessed with all the attributes needed to succeed in fundraising – won't get very far. The reasons are obvious: the world of donors is vast, almost unlimited, and no individual can reach more than a very small section of it. Moreover, fundraisers need the legitimacy provided by having others vouch for them and their organization's work. Friends are an essential and indivisible element of success in resource development. Identifying, recruiting, and nurturing the organization's friends requires considerable skill and understanding and demands a lot of time and energy. But it is utterly indispensable.

9. NURTURE DONORS AND PARTNERS

Nurturing existing friends and donors is the most important task of any fundraising professional. One of the most common mistakes made by organizations is focusing their efforts on bringing in new funders and neglecting funders who have already given to the organization. There are endless examples of this unfortunate behavior.

I once hosted Barbara and Jack, donors from Canada, who shared with me the following story:

> Some twenty-five years ago, we gave $25,000 to a certain university in Israel to establish a new wing of a building. This was a very respectable sum at that time. After we transferred the money, we received a certificate of recognition from the university and a photograph of the sign with our name on the outside of the building. For several years, they kept in touch with us, but over time, the contact died away, and we stopped hearing from the university's representatives in Canada and in Israel. When we came to visit twenty years later, we couldn't even find our sign on the building.

At about the same time we had also donated $5,000 to another university in Israel. Though this was a much more modest gift, the university kept in touch with us over the years, sent us updates on the university's activities and accomplishments, and treated us like real partners.

Now, which of those universities do you think we recently gave a large donation to?!

10. USE YOUR SECRET WEAPON

The tenth principle is the most important. It's your own secret weapon. Your special superpower.

Though this is a book aimed at helping people, especially fundraisers, to learn and adopt the tenets of professional fundraising, I don't believe in learning about fundraising just from reading a book or taking a course. Studying, along with hard-won experience, can give you about 90 percent of the skills you need. But the remaining 10 percent consists of the secret sauce, that magical ingredient that each and every one of us carries within.

In 2006, I was the VP for resource development at Tel Hai College in Israel's far north, the Upper Galilee. The Second Lebanon War, and the thousands of rockets fired from Lebanon into the north of Israel, had shone a national and international spotlight on the region. Suddenly, everyone realized that it was vital to reinforce and develop the Galilee. At Tel Hai, we were ready with a strategic plan for developing the Upper Galilee through a collaborative effort of advanced industry, research, and academia. To that end, we wanted to set up a new campus and shared industrial-research laboratories at a total cost of around $100 million.

With the help of our board chairman, Avraham Shochat, we made contact with the IDB Group, headed by Nochi Dankner. Following the war, IDB had decided to donate 100 million shekels (approximately $25 million) per year to strengthen the periphery. After about six months of discussions with IDB's philanthropic staff, we submitted two requests for funding, of between $500,000 and $700,000. We were then invited to a summit meeting with Dankner himself, who would make the final decision.

The meeting was held far from Israel's northern periphery, at the IDB offices high up in one of Tel Aviv's high-rise towers. Representing the college were the president, the CEO, and myself. On IDB's side of the table were Nochi Dankner and his close assistants, and the staff of the IDB corporate foundation. The meeting began with a routine presentation on the college and then began to drag. At a certain stage, I felt that if we didn't do something drastic, Dankner would lose interest and fall asleep. In preparation for the meeting, I'd tried to study up on Dankner, to understand who he really was and what interested him. Now was the time to put my conclusions into practice.

When the college president came to a pause in his presentation, I jumped to my feet, looked Dankner straight in the eye, and said: "Further to what the president has been saying, I'd like to give you a demonstration of the importance of investing in Tel Hai College as a basis for the development of the entire Upper Galilee. But I'd like to do so using a very different area of expertise – karate."

At this stage, I began to move toward Dankner in karate fighting stance. Keeping my gaze fixed on him, my clenched fists held out in front of my body, I continued: "At karate practice last week, I was talking with my students about a key concept in Japanese called *kime*, which means the concentrated application of force, at the right place and the right time. Understanding *kime* is essential for any karateka to develop and succeed. If IDB wants to strengthen the north in a focused and effective manner – using philanthropic *kime* – then investing in Tel Hai is the best investment you can make."

I concluded this short address with a back-hand strike, accompanied by a loud "kiai!" battle cry, right in front of Dankner's startled face.

The silence was deafening. Everyone in the room was in shock, except for Nochi Dankner. He stood up, smiled, and called to his secretary, who came into the room with a large calendar. He flicked through it and then turned to us: "I'd like to come to the college with my staff to see for myself what you're talking about. Can I visit next Wednesday?"

A week later, he came to Tel Hai with his senior staff. After a work meeting and a tour of the region, he stood with us on the hill of the new campus, asked a few questions, and said with feeling that this was the kind of pioneering venture that needs to be strengthened and nurtured. He then pledged a donation of $2.5 million (which later grew to $3.5 million) to establish the IDB Library, which today is the heart of the new campus.

Everyone has individual abilities, passions, skills, and secret sauce. Fundraising is a profession that requires heart and soul. To be successful, you really have to deploy a wide array of abilities and characteristics – in fact, almost everything you have. Identify your own secret weapon, polish it, and use it mindfully – in the right place and at the right time.

Acknowledgments

I would like to express my sincere thanks and appreciation to the donors, social activists, fundraisers, organization leaders, foundation directors, and many other good and wise men and women who enlightened me and shared their experiences and insights with me along this journey. These include Shai Ben Mordechai, Ori Ben Shlomo, Michael Bohnen, Alan Brown, Shimrit Burla, Julie Council, David Cohen, Perry Davis, Shlomo Dushi, Efrat Duvdevani, Amy Eisenstein, Amos Elad, Per-Ake Eliasson, Bob and Sheila Friedland, Jeremy Friedman, Inbal Freund, Alan Gill, Leo Goldhar, Mark Gurvis, Danny Hakim, Gerry Halbert, Yehuda Halevi, Oren Heiman, Steve Hoffman, Guy Holtzman, Lee Khorman, Warren Kimel, Na'ama Klar, Harvey Kruger, Maya Lapid Edut, Noam Lautman, Eli Lavan, Gilad Maoz, Fadoul Mazawi, Thomas Mullins, Vera Muravitz, Na'ama Or, Limor Regev, Tamara Rogers, Jay Ruderman, Peter Rzepka, Ron Schiller, Lionel Schipper, Natie Shevel, Avraham (Beiga) Shochat, Bob Shook, Barry Shrage, Shoel Silver, Joe Sokol, Ron Solomon, Larry Smith, James Snyder, Isaac Tau, Fred Waks, Philippe Weil, Liat Weiss Shahaf, Robert Zarnegin, and Offi Zisser.

To my publisher, Ilan Greenfield, and my editor, Kezia Raffel Pride, at Gefen Publishing House, for your trust and partnership in making this vision come true.

To my colleagues, teachers, and friends along the way whose love and wisdom I recall frequently: Professor Art Naparstek of blessed memory, Eitan Gedalizon of blessed memory, and Alan Schonberg of blessed memory.

To Gideon Wallis for the special guidance and advice.

To my soulmate and partner Betsy Winnick-Melamed and to our children Guy, Eden, Ari, and Sivan – my advisors, wellspring, strength and motivation.